BURNING WATER

BURNING WATER

Thought and Religion in Ancient Mexico

LAURETTE SÉJOURNÉ

INTRODUCTION BY

JOSÉ A. ARGÜELLES

SHAMBHALA
Berkeley
1976

SHAMBHALA PUBLICATIONS, INC.
2045 Francisco Street
Berkeley, California 94709

Originally published by
The Vanguard Press, 1956.

ISBN 0-87773-090-3
LCC 76-14205

Distributed in the United States by Random House
and in Canada by Random House of Canada Ltd.

Printed in the United States of America.

CONTENTS

FOREWORD
INTRODUCTION

PART I: THE AZTEC EMPIRE

I The Conquest of Mexico 1
II The Nature of Aztec Society 6
III Human Sacrifices 11
IV Sources of the History of Ancient Mexico 16
V The Formation of Aztec Culture 18
VI The Toltecs 21
VII Quetzalcoatl 24
VIII Quetzalcoatl's Betrayal 28
IX Causes of the Fall of the Aztec Empire 43

PART II: THE NAHUATL RELIGION

I Magic 48
II Religion and the Quetzalcoatl Myth 53

PART III: NAHUATL SYMBOLIC LANGUAGE

I Ancient Tollan 80
II Teotihuacan, City of the Gods 84
III The Law of the Centre 89
IV The Paintings of Teotihuacan 94
V Union of Water and Fire 99
VI Union of Heaven and Hell 111
VII The Heart and Penitence 119

Contents

PART IV: THE NAHUATL GODS

I	The Free Spirits	*Page* 130
II	Quetzalcoatl	136
III	Xochipilli, Lord of Souls	144
IV	Xipe Totec, Lord of Liberation	148
V	Huitzilopochtli, The Fifth Sun	156
VI	Tezcatlipoca, Lord of the Smoking Mirror	161
VII	Conclusion	182

INDEX 185

ILLUSTRATIONS

Plates

		Facing Page
1	Teotihuacan: pyramid of the Sun	2
2	Palace of Quetzalcoatl, Teotihuacan	2
3	Platforms and foundations, Quetzalcoatl's palace in Teotihuacan	3
4	The pyramid of Quetzalcoatl	3
5	Carved heads of Quetzalcoatl and of Tlaloc	3
6	Fragment of a reptile from Teotihuacan	18
7	Hieroglyph for a cycle of time	19
8	Knight Eagle	34
9	Aztec drum	35
10	Round temple, Malinalco	50
11	Interior of the temple of Malinalco	50
12	Mayan sculptured stone, Palenque	51
13	Teotihuatecan dancers	66
14	Teotihuatecan dolls	66
15	Teotihuatecan mask	67
16	Chalchiuhtlicue, goddess of rivers	67
17	Xochipilli, Lord of Flowers	82
18	Xipe, the Flayed God	83
19	Coyolxauhqui, Huitzilopochtli's sister	98
20	Coatlicue, the mother goddess	99
21	An image of Quetzalcoatl	114
22	Detail of the back of the sculpture shown in plate 21	115

Illustrations

Line Drawings

Fig.		*Page*
1	Symbol of the Fifth Sun and the sign of Venus	90
2	The five points in a cross or quincunx	91
2a	The five points enclosed in a square	91
3	The quincunx on the headdress of the Fire God	91
4	The Aztec calendar	93
5	The Cross of Quetzalcoatl	95
6	The Cross of Quetzalcoatl on the headdress of a Fire God	95
7	The Cross on Quetzalcoatl's shield	95
8	Eagle bearing the Cross of Quetzalcoatl	95
9	The Cross of Quetzalcoatl in the Codex Borbonicus	96
10	The symbol for Venus	96
11	The hieroglyph *movement*	97
12	Mazapan	99
13	The Terrestrial Paradise	100
14	The Rain God, bearing the Cross of Quetzalcoatl	101
15	The Rain God presiding over the Terrestrial Paradise	102
16	Aquatic signs appearing in Teotihuacan	103
17	Huehueteotl, ancient Fire God	105
18	God of Rain on a Teotihuatecan vase	106
19	Teotihuatecan ceramic stylizations of butterflies	106
20	Sculptured Aztec monument	107
21	Hieroglyph of the burning water	108
22	Quetzalcoatl bearing the hieroglyph *burning water*	109
23	Quetzalcoatl in his aspect of Lord of Dawn	110
24	The Great Temple of Tenochtitlan	111
25	Tiger and coyote representing the Sun and Quetzalcoatl	112
26	The Earth Sun, and Quetzalcoatl in his animal form	113

Fig.		*Page*
27	Symbolic struggle between eagle and tiger	114
28	Solar Eagle	115
29	Teotihuatecan ceramic figure representing an Eagle Knight	116
30	A Knight Eagle	117
31	A Knight Tiger	118
32	Aztec wood carving	119
33	Tiger-Bird-Serpent carved on a Teotihuatecan vase	120
34	Tiger-Bird-Serpent	120
35	Reuniting of the diverse cosmic levels	121
36	Tree of Life from the Codex Borgia	122
37	Symbol for *Tamoanchan*	123
38	Solar Eagle	124
39	The human heart as represented in Teotihuacan	125
40	Cross-section of a human heart	125
41	Obsidian sacrificial knives	125
42	The Lord of Dawn splitting open a human heart	126
43	Images of pierced hearts	127
44	Hieroglyph *movement*	128
45	Emblem of penitence	129
46	Quetzalcoatl bearing the symbol of penitence	131
47	Animal representations	133
48	Teotihuatecan Lord of Earth	134
49	Quetzalcoatl breathing life into a skeleton	135
50	Quetzalcoatl as Wind God	137
51	Teotihuatecan seashell decorated in fresco	138
52	Quetzalcoatl, from a Teotihuatecan fresco	139
53	Lord of Dawn, from a Teotihuatecan fresco	140
54	The reptile superimposed on the Wind God	141
55	Xolotl: the larval form of Quetzalcoatl	143

Fig.		*Page*
56	Xolotl expressing penitence	145
57	Xochipilli, Lord of Flowers	146
58	Xochipilli, Lord of Flowers	147
59	The penitent Xolotl lighting the sun	149
60	Xipe, in a Zapotec ceramic	151
61	Head of the Flayed Lord, Xipe	153
62	Ceramic sculpture of Xipe	155
63	Hieroglyph for gold	161
64	Tezcatlipoca in his Tiger form	162
65	Tezcatlipoca in his Turkey form	163
66	Hieroglyph of the smoking mirror	165
67	A Mayan with the hieroglyph Venus	167
68	Mayan Lord of Dawn, with the hieroglyph Venus	168
69	Hieroglyph of the morning Star	169
70	Venus emerging from a tiger's jaws	170
71	Skull bearing the hieroglyphs *burning water*	171
72	Hand of God	172
73	Hands with drops falling from them	172
74	Divine footprint	173
75	Footprint of the Invisible God	174
76	Hieroglyph *movement* with divine footprints	174
77	Footprints marking out Aztec route	174
78	The hand as a Mayan hieroglyph	175
79	Objects flowing from miraculous hands	175
80	Deity creating the world of forms	176
81	Tiger-Bird-Serpent's breath	177
82	Hand and foot in a composition	179

FOREWORD

AFTER I had sent the manuscript of this book to the publishers, the Mexican Institute of Anthropology and History entrusted me with a grant for excavating in Teotihuacan from October 17, 1955, to February 15, 1956. During these four months a palace, its many rooms and walls all covered with frescoes, made its appearance where previously there had been only a humble bean-field. Tombs and places of worship were also unearthed. The full result of this work will only be known when the findings have been analysed, but it is already certain that the symbolic motifs on the wall paintings and ceramics, together with other traces of a cultural life, fully confirm my thesis as put forward in this book. We have no doubt that, in the light of these new discoveries and of others which will arise and of further excavation this autumn, Teotihuacan will be reinstated as the cradle of Nahuatl civilization, and Pre-columbian religion will be acknowledged to rank among the highest manifestations of the human spirit.

LAURETTE SÉJOURNÉ

Mexico, August 1956

INTRODUCTION

The re-edition of Laurette Séjourné's classic study will be welcomed and appreciated by a generation of readers whose spiritual and cultural awareness has undergone a profound revolution since the book was last issued as a paperback in 1960. During that brief period of time, a tremendous amount of spiritual, philosophical and arcane lore from various traditions—Oriental, European, as well as native American—has come to public attention through an abundance of texts, accompanied by widespread experimentation with psycho-spiritual techniques of all sorts. As much as this revolution of the sacred has begun to alter our styles of life, it has equally started to change and expand our intellectual horizons. Our self-conception has exploded out of the compact little ball of European and orthodox Judeo-Christian world views to include a dramatic reappraisal of the significance of so-called primitive and non-Western cultures, calling into question the entire edifice of modern civilization. In American society this revolution of values has also been represented by a rekindled awareness of cultural origins on the part of minority populations like the Afro-American, Native American and the Mexican-American (Chicano), resulting in the beginnings of a genuine renaissance of indigenous artistic and intellectual activity.

In the context of these far-reaching cultural changes, *Burning Water* should now find an audience who will be able to put it to serious use. With the possible exception of Frank Water's *Mexico Mystique,* no book dealing with the culture and thought of ancient Mexico is as probing as this one. Certainly there is none that is as sensitive to the profound spiritual message and cosmic symbolism of the religion of the plumed serpent, Quetzalcoatl, as Mme. Séjourné's highly informed and impassioned study. The value of this book, which has only increased in time, may be divided into three broad areas of significance. First, the presentation powerfully clears away many major misconceptions about ancient Mexico—misconceptions deriving from a facile identification of Aztec with all things Mexican. As Mme. Séjourné makes clear, the Aztec system of human sacrifice was a tremendous perversion of a mystical perception that had been developed at least a millenium prior to the development of Aztec civilization. The origin of the brilliant, schizophrenically multi-faceted beliefs characterizing Aztec thought and culture was none other than the cosmopolis of Teotihuacan, which Mme. Séjourné identifies with the fabulous, semi-mythical city of Tollan. Her reflections and commentaries on the mytho-historic relationship between earlier and later Mexican civilization will provide the reader with insights suggestive of the universal law and purpose guiding all human cultural development.

In clarifying the fateful ties between the Aztecs and the majestic civilization of Teotihuacan, Mme. Séjourné helps bring into focus the second broad area of significance: the often contradictory aspects of the mythic structure underlying the religion of Quetzalcoatl. Though there may still be points of controversy in her interpretations of Quetzalcoatl, she clearly has brought its mythic dimensions into a perspective where they may stand on a comparable level with the better known mythological, cosmological and religious systems of Europe and the Orient, most notably Christianity and Buddhism. Through her presentation of the complex of astronomical, historical and psychological structures woven around the figure of Quetzalcoatl, Mme. Séjourné has rendered a great service, contributing to our over-all understanding of the universality of the patterns of human thought and spiritual development. It should now be evident that the religion of Quetzalcoatl, long the subject of fantasy and romance (D.H. Lawrence's *Plumed Serpent* readily comes to mind), was a highly inspired system of intuitive thought yielding insights about life, death, and rebirth that provided the basis for a culture—Teotihuacan—that ranks with those of ancient Egypt, and more recently Tibet, in the splendor and integrity of its spiritual purpose.

Behind every great spiritual culture are its mysteries: a unified system of practices and beliefs based upon the wisdom and insights of its most accomplished sages. By far the greatest value and inspiration to be derived from *Burning Water* is the sensitivity with which the author has illumined her third major area of focus, the mysteries of the religion of the Lord of Dawn, Quetzalcoatl. Utilizing indigenous literary sources and extant archaeological material, Mme. Séjourné has vividly recreated the essence of that religion in terms of a few fundamental and universally valid truths: the Law of the Center; the Union of Fire and Water; the Union of Heaven and Hell; and the role and purpose of suffering—the Heart and Penitence. It is this last truth which is the basis of the conception of the Fifth Sun, the Sun of Movement, signifying that sacrifice and transmutation of self or ego without which spiritual realization is impossible. The Aztecs interpreted the meaning of the Fifth Sun literally, thereby inaugurating the institution of human sacrifice. The various mythic and historical dimensions opened up by the mysteries of Quetzalcoatl are written about in a manner that is totally immediate; there can be no doubt regarding Mme. Séjourné's conviction of their value and meaning for ourselves, the actual inhabitants of the Fifth Sun, the Age of the Center. Ultimately, it is this sense of the validity of the intensely spiritual and prophetic nature of the teachings of Quetzalcoatl that imbue *Burning Water* with its most lasting qualities.

The civilization of Teotihuacan and its chief descendent, the Aztec, have long since been overwhelmed by time, but they retain a destiny that is still pregnant with possibility. However, without the continuity of living transmission, spiritual traditions may seem arid and academic. It is only through a reading of symbols that a living quality may be properly transmitted. Mme. Séjourné has been wise in presenting a text that is accompanied by numerous illustrations. For these images, so indispensable to Mme. Séjourné's own analyses, provide the reader with a tangible, aesthetic key for comprehending the message of Quetzalcoatl. The text also illuminates these symbols in such a way that they once again present themselves as images ready to be used by the thoughtful and discriminating artist, mythologist or student of comparative religion. Intuitive reflection upon these symbols may open the doors to further insights connecting and relating the thought and culture of Quetzalcoatl both to other spiritual systems as well as to the needs of the present-day seeker.

With these considerations in mind, the reader may approach this text with the attitude of one about to be revealed a vision of multiple insight and splendor. Through Mme. Séjourné's careful but impassioned efforts, an important aspect of our own history, aesthetic effort, and spiritual development are simultaneously illumined. At their best, books may be bridges across which the consciousness of the individual may be led to a re-evaluation of its own frontiers. *Burning Water* is such a bridge. May the reader, taking this book in hand, delight in the approaching journey.

José A. Argüelles

Berkeley, May 1976

PART I

The Aztec Empire

I

THE CONQUEST OF MEXICO

FROM THE POINT OF VIEW of what we know today, it seems impossible that Europe could have remained completely ignorant until the sixteenth century of a civilization which by that time had existed in Mexico for over fifteen hundred years. Equally surprising is the indifference shown by the conquerors toward the universe it was their fate to stumble upon. Nothing shows Cortés's inner attitude, maintained up to the end of the conquest, better than his gift of glass beads to the Aztec lords: in spite of his surprise at finding signs of great cultural refinement, he never for a moment doubted that he was in the presence of a barbarous people interesting only because they were fabulously wealthy. Nowhere in his writing does he show the least desire to understand them; in fact he condemned them out of hand before he had made more than the most superficial acquaintance with them. Thus only a fleeting glimpse of the ancient civilization was vouchsafed to us before it was reduced to ruins.

Hernán Cortés landed on the coast of Mexico in February 1519. Eight months later he had already reached the heart of the Empire, the fabulous Tenochtitlan, and had been received as a guest of honour.

This triumphal march can be explained mainly by the warrior's undoubted talent for intrigue and betrayal, which enabled him to orientate himself quickly in the maze of native politics. Soon after his arrival he discovered resentment and rebellion simmering among Moctezuma's subject tribes, and at once formed the military alliances that made his dazzling victories possible. An indomitable will, not shrinking from assassination or wholesale massacre, accomplished the rest.

The slaughter he ordered in Cholula, the most important sanctuary in the Pre-columbian world, may even have encouraged Moctezuma's friendly reception of him. A man capable of ordering six thousand throats to be cut in less than two hours—the victims were gathered at the time in a temple patio—must certainly have earned the admiration of that great warrior chief, the Aztec emperor. This exploit, which took place shortly before the arrival of Cortés in the capital, also explains the surprising passivity of the Mexican nobles. It is otherwise incomprehensible that the Spaniards should have been able to stroll about the streets in safety, meeting no opposition, entering the most sacred places and taking measures that were to lead to the overthrow of the Empire, such as capturing Moctezuma in the midst of his own people and destroying the idols which they so fervently worshipped. It was only after a second atrocity as bloody as that of Cholula that the Mexicans finally decided to drive the invaders from the city.

An important religious ceremony was in progress at the time. Attracted by the jewels on the vestments, the Spanish soldiers threw themselves upon a multitude worshipping in the Great Temple patio:

> "... they seized all the patio gates so that none might go out, and others entered with arms and began to kill those that were at the feast, and they cut off the hands and heads of those who played instruments, and stabbed and sent swords through any they met, and caused very great slaughter. Blood ran in the patio like water when it rains . . . the Spaniards searched in every corner for those who were alive, in order to kill them. As the news spread to the city, they gave voice, crying, 'To arms, to arms!' And with the voices came a great crowd of people, all armed, and they began to fight the Spaniards."[1]

1 PYRAMID OF THE SUN, Teotihuacan

2 THE PALACE OF QUETZALCOATL, Teotihuacan, seen from the air

3 PLATFORMS AND FOUNDATIONS of the sanctuaries surrounding Quetzalcoatl's palace in Teotihuacan

4 THE PYRAMID OF QUETZALCOATL, which forms part of his palace. Carvings of the head of the plumed serpent can be seen flanking the steps. Along the platforms at the side they alternate with images of the rain god, Tlaloc

5 CARVED HEADS of Quetzalcoatl and Tlaloc superimposed on serpents bodies in low relief. Details from the pyramid of Quetzalcoatl

After a few days' resistance, the Spaniards were forced to abandon Tenochtitlan, where they had lived peacefully for obout five months. During the retreat many were drowned under the weight of booty they wished to carry with them at all costs.

In order to counter-attack the huge lake city they had to build a number of boats, and thus nearly a year passed in preparations before they were able to return to the assault.

The siege, when it came, lasted seventy-five days. By the time Cuauhtémoc, the emperor who succeeded Moctezuma, had surrendered, Tenochtitlan had ceased to exist. Its burnt temples had been reduced to rubble; its houses, destroyed to obtain material for the landings on the island-city, lay at the bottom of the canals; its inhabitants had been decimated by war, hunger and pestilence.

The survivors tried to flee from the shameful slavery that threatened them, but:

> ". . . the Spaniards and their friends placed themselves on all the roads, and robbed those that passed, seizing the gold and the young and beautiful women . . . they also took youths and strong men as slaves . . . and many of these they branded in the face."[2]

Thus ended the most powerful Empire in all Pre-columbian America.

Native witnesses of the fall have described the dramatic event with great power. Here are two examples from a manuscript written in Nahuatl, the language of the Aztecs, shortly after the conquest:

> "At last we all began to move toward the place where the waters divide, and we arrived at the point of battle. All was confusion there. Only on the high ground did the people take refuge: the waters were full of men, full of men were the roads. Thus did the Mexican end . . . and he left his city abandoned. There where the waters divide we were all re-united. Now we had neither shields nor swords; nothing to eat now, and we ate no more. And thus the whole night it

rained on us. When our chiefs were taken prisoner, that was when the people began to go in search of a place where they might stay. And even as they went, among their rags, in the most secret parts of their bodies and in all places, the conquerors made scrutiny and search; and they unwound the skirts of the women, felt everywhere with their hands, searched in their mouths, their ears, their breasts and hair. And thus was the town invaded and the people scattered on every side; they hid in the corners or near the old walls. In a year 3-House the city fell, so we scattered, in the month when the flowers change, on a day of the sign 1-Snake."[3]

"All this befell us. We saw it, we wondered.
We found ourselves afflicted with ill fortune.
On the roads lie broken arrows,
Hairs are torn out.
The houses are roofless,
Their walls reddened.
Worms multiply in the streets and squares,
Brains are spattered on the walls.
The waters are red as if stained,
And when we drink it is as if we drank salt water.
Meanwhile we laid low the adobe walls
And our heritage was a net of holes.
Shields protected it,
But even shields could not preserve its solitude!
We have eaten of the stalk of the coral tree,
We have chewed salty couch grass,
Lumps of adobe, lizards, mice, the dust of the earth,
worms . . ."[4]

Thus it came about that Tenochtitlan, the centre of the Aztec world, was destined to be known to the west only through the reports of those who destroyed it. Let us turn to these reports, and see what kind of picture they give of this "Mexican Venice".

It was a city of about three hundred thousand inhabitants, built on a lake and joined to the land by three magnificent causeways. Many bridges extended these causeways into the centre of the city.

> ". . . It looked like those enchanted things of which they speak in the book of Amadís; because of its great towers, and pyramids and buildings in the water, all of masonry, some of our soldiers said that surely what they saw was a dream. . . ."[5]

Referring to the great, stone-paved square about the main temple, Bernal Díaz tells us:

> ". . . there were soldiers that had been in many parts of the world, in Constantinople and in all Italy and Rome, and they said they had never seen a square so well proportioned and so orderly and of such a size and so full of people."[6]

The markets, frequented daily by no less than seventy thousand people and brimming with gold, silver, precious jewels, bright-coloured feathers and luxurious tropical fruits, seemed particularly to have fascinated and astonished the Europeans.

Cortés himself gives precise and valuable descriptions of Tenochtitlan:

> ". . . There are in this great city many mosques or houses for their idols, very beautifully built . . . and among these mosques is one, the chief, and no human tongue can describe its size and characteristics; for it is so great, that in its orbit, which is entirely enclosed by a very high wall, a town of five hundred inhabitants could well be built. It contains within this enclosure, all about, very delightful apartments in which there are large rooms and passages where the priests dwell. There are quite forty towers very high and well worked . . . the greatest is higher than the tower of the great church of Seville. They are so well fashioned, of both stone and wood, that they cannot anywhere be better made or fashioned. . . . There are in this great city many very fine and large houses that . . . have very delightful gardens of flowers of different kinds, in the upper floors as well as in those below. Not to be more prolix in telling of the things in this great city . . . I do not wish to say more than that in its amenities and the bearing of its people there is almost the same manner of living as in Spain, and with as much con-

> venience and order as there, and that considering this people to be barbaric and so far from the knowledge of God and communication with other nations possessed of reason, it is an admirable thing to see what they have in all things."[7]

The magnificence of Moctezuma's palaces was such that Cortés confessed himself incapable of attempting a description, and he merely tells his King:

> ". . . it would seem to me wellnigh impossible to tell of their excellence and grandeur . . . and so I shall say nothing about them, only that in Spain there is not their like."[8]

II

THE NATURE OF AZTEC SOCIETY

On what cultural level should we place Aztec society? This is the central problem in Pre-columbian history, and one which has given rise to endless discussion. If we study the conquerors' testimonies closely, we reach the inevitable conclusion that the Aztecs can in no sense be considered barbarians. They possessed, as we shall be able to prove, spiritual riches entitling them to rank with highly civilized peoples.

Contrary to the opinion of many students, who base their opinion on the paralysing notion that all values are relative, it is in fact perfectly possible to judge the spiritual content of a bygone culture. For, of all the qualities man may possess, spirituality is without doubt one of the most easily recognizable.

It is obvious, for instance, that what moves us so deeply in many Pre-Spanish works of art is precisely the transcendental principle within them; for the mere craftsman, however perfectly he knows his job, can never achieve a masterpiece that will overcome the barriers of history and touch the deepest things in us. It is not possible to explain the fascination which the religious centres of ancient Mexico hold even for the most casual visitor, except by recognizing the spiritual qualities that gave rise to their construction and that are still perceptible in their ruins.

There exist documents which, even more than the sculptures and the buildings themselves, reveal the spiritual power that created them. These are the literary fragments that have been miraculously preserved to this day. Whether they are short, casual poems, solemn ceremonial texts, or mythical tales, the fragments are always permeated with a disquietude no different from that which has moved the great religious spirits of all times. Later in this book their composition will be analysed and their authenticity established. We give here a few examples without comment. The first two are songs:

Do I go, perhaps, to my house? Do I go with him,
perhaps?
He came, also, to cut off my life on the earth!
Be thou, god, on my side; mould me!
Recreate thy breast, appease thy heart, make thy heart
glad!

Dost thou think, perhaps, my heart, thou shalt live on
the earth alone?
Thou art anguished, heart of mine. I was born upon
earth.
Art thou thine own friend, perhaps?
Dost thou live perhaps for thyself?
Be thou, god, on my side; mould me!
Recreate thy breast, appease thy heart, make thy heart
glad!

O thou, Acahuitzin, of the turquoise staff:
Crawling I make my way, make my way on the earth!
Be thou, god, on my side; mould me!
Recreate thy breast, appease thy heart, make thy heart
glad!

*

I weep, I grow sad, I am only a singer;
If I could only sometimes carry flowers,

could adorn myself with them in the Place of the
 Fleshless!
I am saddened.
Only as a flower is man honoured upon earth:
an instant so brief he enjoys the flowers of spring:
rejoice with them! I am saddened.
I come from the house of the delicate butterflies:
my song unfolds her petals: behold these myriad flowers:
my heart is a motley painting![9]

We find this same mystic flavour in the texts of discourses given by the Ancients on solemn occasions. Here is one delivered to adolescents about to enter the College where all the high families of the empire were educated:

> ". . . Look thou, son, thou shalt not be honoured, nor obeyed and esteemed, but thou shalt be ordered, thou must be humble and despised and cast down; and if thy body gather to itself strength and pride, punish and humble it; look that thou remember not any carnal thing! . . . Look that thou be not surfeited with food, be temperate, love and practice abstinence and fasting . . . and also, my son, thou must take good care to understand our lord's books; unite thyself with the wise and clever, and those of good understanding . . ."

The following fragment, Sahagún tells us, comes from "the advice . . . of the noble to his sons":

> "Take great pains to make yourselves friends of god who is in all parts, and is invisible and impalpable, and it is meet that you give him all your heart and body, and look that you be not proud in your heart, nor yet despair, nor be cowardly of spirit; but that you be humble in your heart and have hope in God. . . . Be at peace with all, shame yourselves before none and to none be disrespectful; respect all, esteem all, defy no one, for no reason affront any person . . . humble yourselves before all though they say what they like of you; be silent, and though they bring you as low as they please, answer no word . . ."[10]

And here are words to be pronounced by the midwife who offers the newborn child to the goddess of water:

> ". . . Now the child is in your hands, wash and clean him as you know is fitting . . . purify him from the filth he has taken from his parents, and let the water carry away the stains and dirt, and repair them, and clean away all impurity that is in him. Deem it fitting, good Lady, that his heart and life be purified and cleansed . . . in your hands he stays, for you alone are worthy and deserving of the gift you possess to cleanse, from before the beginning of the world."[11]

What proves conclusively, however, that the spiritual development of the Pre-Spanish peoples had reached a high level is the existence among them of the concepts of baptism and the forgiveness of sins. Though evidence for this is usually looked upon with indifference by investigators, as if they were just simple rituals among many others, these sacraments imply an unsuspected level of inner development: purification and humility being the fundamentals of any true religious life.

As this point is so important for an understanding of Aztec thought, we quote part of the sermon the confessor directs to the penitent. The words, says Sahagún, are "from the oral confession these natives use at the time of their infidelity, once in their lives":

> ". . . the confessor speaks to the penitent saying: 'Oh brother, thou hast come to a place of great danger, and of much work and terror . . . thou hast come to a place where snares and nets are tangled and piled one upon another, so that none can pass without falling into them . . . these are thy sins, which are not only snares and nets and holes into which thou hast fallen, but also wild beasts, that kill and rend the body and the soul. . . . When thou wast created and sent here, thy father and mother Quetzalcoatl made thee like a precious stone . . . but by thine own will and choosing thou didst become soiled . . . and now thou hast confessed . . . thou hast uncovered and made manifest all thy sins to our lord who shelters and purifies all sinners; and take not this

as mockery, for in truth thou hast entered the fountain of mercy, which is like the clearest water with which our lord god, who shelters and protects us all, washes away the dirt from the soul . . . now thou art born anew, now dost thou begin to live; and even now our lord god gives thee light and a new Sun; now also dost thou begin to flower, and to put forth shoots like a very clean precious stone issuing from thy mother's womb where thou art created. . . . It is fitting that thou do penance working a year or more in the house of god, and there shalt thou draw blood, and shalt pierce thy body with cactus thorns; and that thou make penance for the adulteries and other filth thou hast done, thou shalt pass osiers twice a day, one through thine ears and one through thy tongue; and not only as penance for the carnal sins already mentioned, but also for words and injuries with which thou hast affronted and hurt thy neighbours, with thy evil tongue. And for the ingratitude in which thou hast held the favours our lord hast done thee, and for thy inhumanity to thy neighbours in not making offering of the goods bestowed upon thee by god nor in giving to the poor the temporal goods our lord bestowed upon thee. It shall be thy duty to offer parchment and copal, and also to give alms to the needy who starve and who have neither to eat nor drink nor to be clad, though thou know how to deprive thyself of food to give them, and do thy best to clothe those who go naked and in rags; look that their flesh is as thine, and that they are men as thou art."[12]

Anticipating the incredulity that might greet these testimonies of the undoubted spirituality of the people they had come to convert, the good Father Sahagún declared in the prologue to his sixth book:

"... what is written down in this volume, no human being would have sufficient understanding to invent, nor could any living man contradict the language that therein is, so that if all the Indians who understand these things were questioned, they would affirm that this is the language proper to their ancestors and the works they did."

Surprising as it may seem, no attempt has been made to explain the origin of confession among the natives, though this is so important a spiritual phenomenon that it might well be supposed to contain the key to their secret religious system.

The chief reason for such negligence may be the disconcerting ambiguity of Aztec culture. Side by side with manifestations of undeniable moral greatness are signs of extreme barbarity, such as the human sacrifices round which Aztec life revolved, and which have unfortunately discouraged all desire to understand. Anyone trying to study Aztec thought comes sooner or later upon this deep contradiction, which, unless the reasons for it are understood, is apt to be resolved by intellectual sleight-of-hand with resulting confusion.

III

HUMAN SACRIFICES

It must be admitted that ritual killing seems to have been a greater need in Tenochtitlan than the will to purity implicit in penance and baptism. The annals tell us proudly of the tens of thousands of victims whose hearts were torn out on solemn occasions. In fact sacrifice formed an integral part of daily life, on the one hand because it was the central point of the ceremonies that so completely absorbed the population, on the other because individuals had the right to sacrifice on their own account. For example, a rich merchant who gave a banquet could well afford the luxury of buying slaves in order to have them killed by a priest and then to share the cooked morsels among his guests. Here is what Sahagún says on the subject:

> ". . . They used to buy these slaves in Azcapotzalco because there is a fair where those who deal in such vile merchandise sell. . . . The dealer who buys and sells slaves hires singers to sing and play . . . so that the slaves shall dance and sing in the square. . . . Those wishing to buy slaves for sacrifice and for eating go there to watch them as they dance, well

groomed; and the one who sings best and dances with most feeling to the music and who has a pleasing face and disposition, without physical blemish, and who is not crooked, nor too fat, but well proportioned and fine of stature . . . is bartered for; and those who neither sing nor dance with feeling, they sell for thirty *mantas*, and those who do and who have a pleasant disposition, they sell for forty *mantas*. . . . Returning to his house, the buyer throws them into prison for the night, and in the morning brings them out, and is careful of the women that they spin till the time comes to kill them, but the men are given no work at all. . . . They adorn and dress the slaves that are to die. . . . Being dressed, at midnight, they place them in the porch of the entrance gate so that the guests may see them. . . . All night the visitors to the house eat and drink. . . . On the following day they do the same. . . . They place headdresses of rich feathers on the slaves that are about to die. . . . Then they set guards over them day and night. . . . He who gives the banquet, the fourth time he invites his guests, kills the slaves. . . ."[13]

The endless feasts celebrated the year round were no more than a series of atrocities, and of course the temples looked like slaughter houses. Here is the testimony of one of the conquerors:

"There were a number of braziers containing copal incense, and three hearts of Indians they had sacrificed that day were burning. . . . And all the walls of the temple were so black with scabs of blood, and the floor also, that it stank very evilly."[14]

But nothing gives a more precise picture of the rôle of human sacrifice in Aztec society than the bare list of rituals with which the ruling divinity was celebrated every twenty days:

". . . On the calends of the first month . . . they killed many children, sacrificing them in many places and on the hill tops, removing their hearts in honour of the gods of water. . . .

. . . On the first day of the second month they held a feast in

> honour of the god named Totec . . . in which they killed and flayed many slaves and captives. . . .
>
> . . . On the first day of the third month they held a feast to the god named Tlaloc. . . . At this feast they killed many children in the hills. . . .
>
> . . . On the first day of the fourth month they held a feast in honour of the corn god . . . and killed many children. . . .
>
> . . . In the fifth month they held a great feast in honour of the god called . . . Tezcatlipoca . . . in his honour they killed at the feast a chosen youth who had no blemish on his body. . . .
>
> . . . In the sixth month . . . they killed many captives and other slaves, decked with those ornaments of the gods called Tlaloques. . . .
>
> . . . In the seventh month . . . they held a feast to the goddess of salt . . . in honour of this goddess they killed a woman decked with the ornaments they painted on the goddess herself. . . ."[15]

And so on through the eighteen months of their year. No more details are necessary, this short list being in itself enough to show how difficult it is to judge impartially a society which perpetrates such horrors.

How, after all this, can we take Aztec spirituality seriously? Should we not rather condemn such people once for all as primitive barbarians? We confess that after reading the descriptions of their ceremonies we might be inclined to do so. But then what of the irrefutable evidences of moral striving? Shall we be content with the easy answer, that spiritual values are in any case but relative, and resign ourselves to forgiving the massacres in the name of some obscure justification that escapes our modern understanding? This does not seem an acceptable solution. Whatever its form, the slaughter of human beings is in essence so opposed to spirituality that it is only in the exact measure in which the one is eliminated that the other becomes possible. To confuse Aztec mass extermination with the ethical ideals set forth in their texts would be like explaining away the Inquisition because it emanated from the Church. Some well-meaning research workers have tried to justify these human sacrifices by reminding us of the wars ravaging the world today. Such an argument seems beside the point. It is not a matter of comparing one inhuman act with another, but of understanding how such acts could be officially possible in a society governed by a code forbidding them.

The problem seems not to have worried most students of American history, who have tended to accept with disconcerting ease the explanation of human sacrifice which has been given by the chroniclers.

According to Aztec religion, so these chroniclers tell us and the historians echo, man has no other aim on earth but to feed the Sun with his own blood, without which the sun will die of exhaustion. This tragic dilemma obliges him to choose between indulging in massacre or bringing about the end of the world. So each victim, aware of his cosmic mission, cheerfully allowed his heart to be torn out; and (our own history books are full of parallel examples) the Aztec chroniclers preserved the names of certain warriors whose specially heroic deaths were held up for emulation. But if we do not passively accept these official declarations, if we refuse to regard it as natural that customs should be perpetuated which, whatever their time and place, are monstrous, we may begin to perceive that we are here dealing with a totalitarian state of which the philosophy included an utter contempt for the individual.

If matters were in fact so simple, however, how are we to account for the degree of authority and implacable discipline that ruled in Tenochtitlan? According to the testimony of all the chroniclers, Spanish and native alike, it appears on the surface that any freedom of thought or action was inconceivable in the Aztec world. Laws, penalties, and innumerable prohibitions, indicated to each person in detail the behaviour he must follow in all circumstances of his life; in such a system personal decision did not exist, dependence and instability were absolute, fear reigned. Death lurked ceaselessly everywhere, and constituted the cement of the building in which the individual Aztec was prisoner.

There were those who, by their social status, were by law destined to extermination: the slaves—and anyone might become one through losing his fortune or civic rights; captive warriors; children born beneath a sign favourable for sacrifice and offered to the gods. Capital punishment was another constant threat: to anyone who dared without authority to wear a garment that reached below the knee; to the official who ventured into a forbidden room of the palace; the merchant whose riches had made him too proud; the dancer taking a false step. . . .

Judging by the laws the rulers were apparently obliged to pass, this mechanism for breaking men down was not established as easily as might be supposed. We know, for example, that every person—priest or spectator—who retired from the ceremony before the child-sacrifices to Tlaloc had been consummated was held to be despicable, declared unworthy of all public office, and converted into a wretch without the law. We cannot just be satisfied by explanations which talk of "mysterious magic rituals". Sahagún throws interesting light on the picture when he tells us that:

> "the parents of the victims submitted to these practices, shedding many tears and with great sorrow in their hearts."[16]

The chronicler Tezozmoc describes how the chiefs and lords were invited to witness the human sacrifices on pain of being sacrificed themselves if they did not attend. There were, besides, precautionary measures in case those who went to the sacrifice, instead of climbing the temple steps happily as the moral directive prescribed, had the bad taste to be seized with panic, to faint or weep.

These texts represent authentic human cries and show clearly what struggles and resistence undoubtedly resulted from such a system of terror, the perfection of which causes us all too easily to forget the individual. They show that so-called Aztec religious concepts were little more than a political weapon in the hands of the despots who promulgated them.

How could it be otherwise? Can we seriously believe that any religion—that is, a revelation to free man from the anguish of his destiny—can be built upon laws of human destruction? If it is admitted that a religious doctrine could arise out of a concept so lacking in love—and this not only in the acts of the administrators, which would not surprise us, but in its very origin—then all possibility of understanding has been removed.

How can we suppose that belief in the Sun's tyranny over physical life could have taken such root in human hearts? It is more likely that it could only have been planted there by force. Clearly, the spirituality of some aspects of Aztec life must have sprung from an old pre-Aztec tradition, later betrayed in its most sacred essence so that the interests of a temporal structure ruled by an implacable will to power might be upheld. A careful reading of the historic texts confirms this view.

IV

SOURCES OF THE HISTORY OF ANCIENT MEXICO

Let us now examine the material which makes a history of ancient Mexico possible.

First we have the narratives of the conquerors themselves, the most important being those of Hernán Cortés and Bernal Díaz del Castillo. Besides a detailed account of the conquest, we find in their writings valuable descriptions of the Pre-columbian world, and these men were the only ones who were acquainted with the civilization while it was still alive. As we have already said, the city of Tenochtitlan, which did not surrender until totally annihilated, is known only through their descriptions.

Then there are the documents written by those who, from memory and what ruins remained, tried to evoke the image of this civilization that had been lost for ever. Among these were various natives who, already part of the strange universe of colonial Catholicism, told the history of their past so their new masters may appreciate its greatness. These descendants of princes—Ixtlilxochitl, Tezozmoc, Chimalpaín—transcribed in their own Nahuatl tongue (using our system of phonetic spelling, that is, translating Nahuatl sounds into the Latin alphabet) manuscripts from old royal libraries, for luckily by long-established tradition the pre-Spanish peoples were accustomed to set down the sum total of their knowledge in symbolic ideographic writing.

Another source of knowledge exists in the songs by which in Aztec schools the stories of the gods and heroes were impressed on children's memories. Many of the anonymous manuscripts of the sixteenth and beginning of the seventeenth centuries are simply transcriptions in Nahuatl of myths, epic fragments, or religious poems that had remained alive in some men's hearts. For instance, the work from which any study of pre-Spanish culture must take most of its documentation—that of Bernardino de Sahagún, 1499-1590—was compiled mainly with the help of people who still remembered what had been taught them orally in their youth. As most of our quotations come from Sahagún's monumental work—*History of the Things of New Spain*—it seems useful here to refer to the way in which it was compiled. Nothing could better establish the authenticity of its contents than the precision of the author's investigations. We quote from an eminent authority:

> ". . . four centuries ago this extremely wise Franciscan undertook for the first time in history the most complete ethnographic investigation of any people. . . . His wonderful intuition astonishes us when we realize the *scientific method* he used. Choosing first the best informants, carefully selected for their science and probity, and then succeeding in getting them to relate frankly all they knew; allowing them to give their information in the way easiest and most accessible to them, and as they were most accustomed to—in

> indigenous paintings; using at the same time, as invaluable aids, his ancient native disciples . . . who besides knowing their own language very well, were versed in Latin and Castilian; and finally passing all the information thus gathered through various sieves . . . Sahagún followed . . . the most rigorous and exacting of scientific anthropological methods. . . ."[17]

If to this perspicacity and intellectual probity we add devotion to scientific proof and a profound sympathy for the conquered people, we can see that Sahagún's work constitutes one of the most generous manifestations of the human spirit; it appears, miraculously, to compensate for the lack of human values inherent in any war of conquest.

V

THE FORMATION OF AZTEC CULTURE

In order to analyse Aztec culture correctly we shall have to study its origins. A brief survey of the historical facts is therefore necessary.

From the eleventh century onwards nomad tribes had begun to penetrate the heart of Mexico where, ever since the beginnings of the Christian era, a very high civilization had existed.

The origin of these tribes, all belonging to the large group known as *Chichimeca*—a term designating a primitive state of culture—has not yet been exactly determined. It is commonly believed that they migrated from the north.

The period extending from the eleventh to the beginning of the fourteenth century is dealt with briefly by the chroniclers, who tell us only how these various nomad tribes were converted into agricultural communities and who speak of bloody struggles for possession of the Valley of Mexico, the name given to the high plateau on which Mexico City is now situated.

Among these hunting tribes were the Aztecs. They reached the plateau after laborious wanderings, certain episodes of

6 FRAGMENT OF A REPTILE (probably the tail of a rattlesnake) from the base of the pyramid of the Sun at Teotihuacan

7 HIEROGLYPH FOR A CYCLE OF TIME. Mexican National Museum

which, while suggesting that the migrants lived primitively, strongly emphasize the already specifically warlike characteristics of the future founders of Tenochtitlan. Among these episodes the most significant is undoubtedly that concerning the suppression of the witch who had until then been chief of the tribe, in favour of the hero Huitzilopochtli. It is said that Malinalxochitl, sister of Huitzilopochtli, governed by magic powers of which only she held the secret. Among other alarming talents, she knew how to tame wild beasts, which she afterwards used for causing harm to men. In spite of the adoration and fear which she inspired, her people ended by rebelling against her tyranny, and Huitzilopochtli, appearing in dreams to the priest who had consulted him, advised them to do away with the witch forthwith, declaring that no such old-fashioned methods of sorcery or magic could bring them glory and power, "but only strength and valour of heart and arm."[18]

This event, the culmination of a fight against out-of-date concepts, was a revolution indeed. Assuming will power to be the only possible magic, the participants in the episode seem to have wished to differentiate themselves proudly from the animal and vegetable kingdoms with which they had till then been closely linked, and they substituted the war chief for the sorceress. So it appears that, up to the time they made contact with the religious beliefs of the plateau, the Aztecs knew only the ancient laws of witchcraft. Their new beliefs were immediately adapted to their primitive mentality.

> "My chief mission and my task is war . . . I have to watch and join issue with all manner of nations, and that not kindly."[19]

These words, spoken by Huitzilopochtli after his victory over the witch, Malinalxochitl, before a small group of naked men who shared with him the conquest of the world, mark the beginning of a dramatic human adventure. Filled with the sense of the mission they had to accomplish, the Aztecs advanced along the road indicated by their chief, unhesitating, never pausing to rest, like sleepwalkers; and never for a moment did they seem to forget this terrible prophecy:

> ". . . The four corners of the world shall ye conquer, win, and subject to yourselves . . . it shall cost you sweat, work and pure blood. . . ."[20]

When they came into contact with other peoples, they sternly applied this philosophy of will to power.

Late arrivals in the Valley of Mexico, they at once set to fighting cruelly for the land and for political dominance over the tribes which, having adopted more civilized customs, let themselves be caught unaware by the newcomers' brutality. Piling one atrocity upon another, the Aztecs imposed themselves first upon the communities of the plateau, then upon the whole country, including Central America; till the kingdom of the chosen people, the dream of a few fanatics, became a reality.

Founded precariously in 1325 by a miserable, persecuted people, Tenochtitlan soon became the metropolis the Spaniards later so marvelled at. Engrossed in describing this mad race for power—warlike atrocities, alliances and unions between enemies, betrayals in the name of friendship—the chroniclers scarcely troubled themselves over the more transcendental phenomena of this turbulent period of history, namely the slow integration of the Chichimecas into the cultural complex centred on the plateau. Only through random traces can we piece together for ourselves a picture of how these various primitive hunting peoples became gradually possessed of the rich tradition in which the whole region was steeped. It would appear that the change came about mainly through the women belonging to the civilization that had disintegrated, whom the newcomers took as wives or teachers for their young. We are told, for instance, how, while they were in process of adopting the customs of the ancient culture, at a certain moment they learned to cook the meat they had previously eaten raw; or how they abandoned their caves to live in structures built by hand. They finally assimilated the old language and beliefs to such an extent that after a few generations had gone by they had forgotten their obscure origins, and the chiefs of the various tribes had proclaimed themselves descendants of the glorious people who had flourished in these same parts in olden times. If we remember that not one of these tribes possessed a cultural past, we can easily understand how they may have begun to think that it was their own ancestors who had bequeathed them the basis of their spiritual life.

Naturally, once they had become undisputed masters, the Aztecs established themselves as official heirs to the old civilization; there is no doubt that the power which they received from this spiritual heritage helped them, as much as the bow and arrow, to gain the temporal power—a thing they had so longed to do. The rapid assimilation, by men who had only yesterday been primitive, of a thought, a science, and a highly elaborate medium of expression, once again shows the extraordinary strength of will that infused this short-lived Aztec society.

In tracing Aztec origins, the chroniclers speak of the ancient Nahuas and attribute to them the foundation, at about the beginning of the Christian era, of the religious system that nourished Pre-Columbian Mexico up to the conquest, that is, for fifteen hundred years. And we shall see in another chapter that archaeological excavations have fully confirmed the accuracy of these texts, having unearthed in the ruins of the first Nahuatl capital evidence of the same gods, the same rituals, the same symbolic language as in the last—ill-fated Tenochtitlan.

VI

THE TOLTECS

The veneration shown by the proud Aztecs toward these ancestral Nahuas is certainly surprising. We might have supposed that, once lords of the universe, as it seemed to them, they would have taken full possession of the cultural heritage they had adopted, attributing it perhaps to some national hero. Nothing of the kind happened, because they recognized that their entire system of knowledge came from those who were "the first inhabitants of this land, and the first that came to these parts called the land of Mexico . . . those who first sowed the human seed in this country."[21]

Here we come face to face with this ancient people, whom all documents without exception present as creators of the most important of the ancient cultures. It is said that because of their supreme artistic talents they were called *Toltecs*, a word which in Nahuatl means *master craftsmen*. Let us see what Sahagún says on this subject:

> ". . . Whatever they turned their hands to was delicate and elegant, all was very good, remarkable and gracious, such as the houses they made very beautifully, highly decorated within, of a certain kind of precious stone very green with lime, and those so adorned had a lime highly polished which was a sight to be seen, and stones also, fashioned and stuck together, that seemed like a kind of mosaic; with justice were they later called exquisite and noteworthy, because they possessed such beauty of workmanship and labour. . . .
>
> . . . They were the inventors of the art of featherwork . . . and all that was done in ancient times was made with wonderful invention and great skill.
>
> . . . the Toltecs had much experience and knowledge in the qualities and virtues of herbs, and they left docketed and named those now used for treating, because they were also physicians and the best in the art . . . they were the first inventors of medicine. . . .
>
> . . . What they achieved in knowledge of precious stones was so great that, though these were buried in a larger one and below ground, by their natural genius and philosophy they would discover where to find them. . . .
>
> . . . So remarkable were these Toltecs that they knew all mechanical skills, and in all of these were unique and exquisite craftsmen, for they were painters, stone workers, carpenters, bricklayers, masons, workers in feather and ceramics, spinners and weavers. . . .

. . . They were so skilled in astronomy . . . that they were the first to take count of and order the days of the year. . . .
. . . They also invented the art of interpreting dreams, and they were so informed and so wise that they knew the stars in the heavens and had given them names and knew their influences and qualities. So also they knew the movements of the heavens, by the stars. . . .
. . . These Toltecs were good men and drawn to virtue . . . they were tall, larger in body than those who live now. . . . They also sang well, and while they sang or danced they used drums and timbrels of wood . . . they played, composed and arranged curious songs out of their heads; they were very devout, and great orators. . . ."[22]

This description enumerates the chief characteristics of the more developed Meso-american civilizations and could well serve to define their cultural styles. Yet, extensive as it may seem, the list does not tell of all the skills used in the creation of the great Tollan of legendary splendour. Though what Sahagún tells us is confirmed by archaeological findings, the illustrious historian, who was not privileged to look upon the ruins, is very far from giving us an idea of the prodigious creative power of their builders, which we shall see later for ourselves.

Toltec civilization spread to very distant countries, and it has been proved archaeologically that from the end of the fifth century, that is, about four hundred years after the foundation of its capital, the vast culture-complex had already taken shape and extended more or less over the territories which present-day anthropologists call Meso-america. This fact is also confirmed by historical texts, as can be seen from the following quotation from Sahagún:

". . . such remarkable and elegant things have been found not only in the town of Tollan, but also in all parts of New Spain where their works have been discovered; for example pots . . . children's dolls, jewels and many other things made by them; for these Toltecs have spread almost everywhere. . . ."[23]

Leaving till later the geographical details of this expansion, we will here say only that if we compare this quotation with the corresponding archaeological material, we shall be surprised at the precision of Sahagún's details. As he says, there are few places in Mexico and Central America that do not possess Toltec remains; moreover the objects he names as characteristic of these people are exactly those which have been found during excavations in the ancient capital, including the "children's dolls" which, without this scientific proof, would have seemed a mere fancy of Sahagún's informant.

Years later the Aztecs tried to imitate this unified complex; and the fact that they shared with the lands they coveted the same Toltec cultural heritage no doubt greatly facilitated the task of their diplomats and warriors. Ixtlixochitl confirms this supposition when he says that the Aztecs:

> ". . . had conquered the whole Empire of this New Spain, from the boundaries of the Chichimecas and the kingdom of Michoacan to the farthest provinces possessed by the ancient Toltec kings."[24]

Undoubtedly the Nahuatl influence which in the sixteenth century was found all over the country must have come originally from the Toltecs, and not, as is generally supposed, from the Aztecs. In fact it is highly improbable that in less than a hundred years the latter could have established an alien culture firmly among the conquered peoples who had always regarded them as enemies and who were later to betray them to the Spaniards; especially since the Aztecs rarely occupied the conquered countries, but merely visited them when tribute was not paid promptly enough.

VII

QUETZALCOATL

What made it possible for the Toltecs to achieve their unparalleled greatness? This is a question that cannot be answered fully. Even if we had exact details of the origins of their cultural characteristics—and unfortunately we have not—we would still remain ignorant of the origin of that spiritual spark which alone can light a civilization and which no purely intellectual analysis can explain. But, as we must make some effort to understand, let us examine the facts we actually have at our disposal.

A figure exists who, since he is inextricably linked with Toltec life, may give us a clue. This is Quetzalcoatl. His historical reality seems to be established without doubt, since his qualities as leader are many times mentioned. Sahagún says that:

> ". . . In this city [of Tollan] reigned many years a king called Quetzalcoatl. . . . He was exceptional in moral virtues . . . the place of this king among these natives is like King Arthur among the English. . . ."[25]

But the fame of Quetzalcoatl spread far beyond his ancient capital. In fact he was the central figure in all Meso-american history. No other name, even the most powerful emperor's, is even distantly comparable to his. As an eminent American historian tells us, Quetzalcoatl is:

> ". . . the greatest figure in the ancient history of the New World, with a code of ethics and love for the sciences and the arts."[26]

His essential rôle as founder of Nahuatl culture was never questioned by any of the historians of the sixteenth and seventeenth centuries, who always state that, just as our era began with Christ, so that of the Aztecs and their predecessors began —approximately at the same time—with Quetzalcoatl. His image, the plumed serpent, had for Pre-columbian peoples the same evocative force as has the Crucifix for Christianity. Later, in Tenochtitlán, he continued to be the object of the deepest veneration. Besides being invoked as the creator of man and his work, he was patron of two institutions which were the foundations of all Aztec social and religious life: the priesthood and the college of princes. Until the fall of the Empire the great pontiffs of the metropolis continued to call themselves "successors to Quetzalcoatl".

Who, then, was this primordial figure, and why was his memory so ardently worshipped? As we know that during his reign the first great Pre-columbian city was founded, and that there the social and religious views that dominated Mesoamerica for over fifteen hundred years were crystallized, we must think of him first as an organizer without equal.

But whence did this statesman derive the power which enabled him to amalgamate and transfigure the cultural elements he had inherited from archaic times into so dynamically homogeneous a system? He must evidently have been possessed of some quite exceptional interior strength, and all that is known about him corroborates this view. Summarizing what the chroniclers say on the subject, Alfonso Caso gives us this significant picture:

> ". . . Quetzalcoatl appears as god of life, constant benefactor of humanity, and so we see that, after having created man with his own blood, he searches for a way to nourish him, and discovers the maize that the ants have hidden inside a mountain, and turns himself into an ant and steals a grain which he afterwards gives to men. He teaches them how to polish jade and the other precious stones and how to find where these stones lie; how to weave many-coloured fabrics, with a miraculous cotton that exists already dyed in different colours, and how to make mosaics with *quetzal* plumes, from the bluebird, the humming bird, the parrot and other birds of bright plumage. But above all he taught man science, showing him the way to measure time and study the revolution of the stars; he showed him the calendar and invented ceremonies and fixed the days for prayers and sacrifice."[27]

It would be difficult to place Quetzalcoatl more unequivocally at the very source of all spiritual life, and here, certainly, lies the reason why he is considered above all as a god-man.

The documents relating to his activities as king of Tollan all speak of him as a leader of very high moral standing, whose chief characteristics are essentially religious in nature; and the humility and burning need for purification expressed in certain official Aztec texts clearly emanate from his doctrine.

It is obvious, for instance, that the mystic inspiration pervading the sermon addressed to young nobles entering the Calmecac, a college under the auspices of Quetzalcoatl, could not have sprung from a society which, like that of the Aztecs, dedicated the two centuries of its existence to bloody conquests. On the other hand it is clearly stated that prayer and penitence formed the very nucleus of Quetzalcoatl's teaching. Deep wisdom is also evident in the text describing the election of a high dignitary:

> "He who was perfect in all the customs, exercises and doctrines used by the ministers of the idols, they elected as high pontiff, whom they called king or lord, and all the chiefs called him Quetzalcoatl. . . . In the election no attention was paid to lineage, but only to the customs and exercises, doctrine and good life; whether the high priests possessed these, whether they lived chastely and kept all the customs of the ministers of the idols; he was elected who was virtuous, humble, and peace-loving, and considerate, and prudent, and not frivolous but grave and austere, and jealous of custom, and loving and merciful and compassionate and a friend of all, and devout, and fearful of god. . . . From these priests, the best were elected as high pontiffs and were called . . . successors to Quetzalcoatl. . . ."[28]

Everything that is known about the Aztecs suggests that a character of such virtue would have been troublesome at the head of so cruel an empire. Even if native historians had not so firmly held that all spiritual virtues had been bequeathed to the Aztecs by Quetzalcoatl, we would suspect as much. The contrast between the social reality and the superimposed ethical ideal of Tenochtitlan is the strongest evidence of the power of a message which, fifteen hundred years after its revelation, still represented the only moral basis of life, even though it existed only theoretically.

It is difficult to detect at what point the power of the message began to fade. It can perhaps be truly said that until the eighth century, when owing to a devastating fire, the old Toltec metropolis was abandoned, this pure concept still illumined the great Tollan; but it is impossible to reconstruct the steps that later led to the degeneration in Tenochtitlan.

All that can be said is that the laws of interior preparation revealed by Quetzalcoatl were used by the Aztecs to prop up their bloody State. The mystic union with the divinity, which the individual could achieve only by successive steps and after a life of contemplation and penitence, was thenceforth considered to be the result merely of the manner of a man's death. We are here dealing with low witchcraft: the material transmission of human energy to the sun. The exalted revelation of the eternal unity of the spirit was converted into a principle of cosmic anthropophagy. The liberation of the individual, the separate "I", came to be understood with crude literalness only, and achieved through ritual killings, which in their turn fomented wars.

VIII

QUETZALCOATL'S BETRAYAL

As seems usual in despotic systems, the Aztec state was founded on a spiritual inheritance which it betrayed and transformed into a weapon of worldly power. Considering that the intellectual level of these nomadic hunters must have been very primitive (we remember that shortly before their arrival on the plateau the Aztecs were still ruled by a witch) the metamorphosis of high mystic thought into barbarous magic appears quite natural.

Apart from the easily detectable traces of Quetzalcoatl's doctrine, the Aztecs possessed no belief that can be called religious, and every philosophical or moral concept expressed in their texts is clearly related to the spiritual complex of the Toltecs. The only deity of Aztec origin is Huitzilopochtli, god of war; but, as with all the others, it is impossible to define his characteristics without recourse to the teaching of Quetzalcoatl. In the person of Huitzilopochtli they merely illustrated the mystic principle of integration into a great whole, the principle being represented by a solar being who fed on mortal blood; in other words, the change was merely one of ritual.

Thus it can be affirmed that the ancient tradition was the only spiritual framework of Aztec society. It is astonishing to see how faithfully a tradition was maintained—through prayers, ceremonies, sermons, poems, mythical tales—which reality belied. They continued, for instance, invoking "Our Lord, most humane, protector and helper of all", while in order to feast any one of those "most humane" gods they committed indescribable atrocities, of which the following texts give some idea:

> "They made a very solemn feast to the god called Xipetotec, and also in honour of Huitzilopochtli. At this feast they killed all the prisoners, men, women and children. . . . The owners of the prisoners handed them over to the priests at the foot of the temple, and they dragged them by the hair, each one his own, up the steps; and if they did not wish to go by the steps, they dragged them to the block of stone where they were to kill them, and taking from each one his heart . . . they hurled their bodies down the steps, where other priests flayed them. . . . After they had been flayed, the old men . . . carried the bodies to the CALPULCO where the owner of the captive had made his offering . . . there they dismembered them and sent a limb to Moctezuma to eat, and the rest they shared among the other chiefs and relatives. . . ."[29]
>
> ". . . Each of the nobles took his captive by the hair, and dragged him to a place called Aperlac, and there left him; then they brought those they were to cast into the fire, and they sprinkled their faces with incense . . . they took and bound their hands behind, and also their feet; then they threw them over their shoulders and carried them to the top

of the temple, where was a great fire and a great heap of coals; and when they had arrived at the top, they gave them to the fire . . . and there in the fire the unhappy prisoner began to twist and to retch . . . and he being in such agony, they brought him out with grappling irons . . . and placed him on the stone . . . and opened his breast . . . and took out the heart and threw it at the feet of the statue of Xiuhtecutli, god of fire."[30]

We should here remember that the high priest who fulfilled such tasks had to be, according to official declarations, "virtuous, humble, and peace-loving, and considerate, and prudent, and loving and compassionate and a friend of all, and devout. . . ."

As we know, too, that this pontiff was considered to be a reincarnation of Quetzalcoatl—bright guide of interior perfection—it seems no exaggeration to use the word "betrayal" when we speak of the so-called Aztec religion.

Tenochtitlan relied for its existence upon the tributes from conquered nations, and we can well understand the Aztecs' over-riding need for a system of thought to support their aggressive imperialism. There is no doubt that "the cosmic need for human sacrifice" was an ideal "slogan", for in its name they could wage the innumerable wars which made up their history and consolidated their reign of terror.

By rigorous methods and by discipline they extracted precious materials from the various regions, and fabulous riches flowed into the imperial capital.

Large caravans of tributaries arrived in the city after month-long journeys, bearing cargoes of gold, jade and turquoise all finely worked; dazzling feathers; skins of tiger, lion and leopard, sea shells, salt, cocoa, tobacco. . . .

They also brought copal for the rituals; eagles, puma and serpents for the king's zoological gardens; dwarfs, hunchbacks and albinos for service in the palace; virgins destined for the "house of pleasure", an institution patronized by Huitzilopochtli and devoted to "attracting new souls".

But nothing gives a more vivid picture of the implacable nature of Aztec power than the blood tribute imposed upon Tlaxcala, a neighbour city.

The victories of the people of Tenochtitlan, dedicated exclusively to war, were an obstacle to any new wars because the provinces that still remained to be conquered were separated from the metropolis by subjected territories. True, they counted on punitive expeditions against countries who had the audacity to try and free themselves from the protection of the "chosen people", but these were only isolated cases, insufficient to keep the turbulent Aztec youth fighting fit.

Besides, Huitzilopochtli had declared that he was none too pleased with the sacrifice of barbarians from distant lands, and the high dignitaries of Tenochtitlan thought up the ingenious plan of instituting in Tlaxcala "military fairs" which would allow them to offer victims as appetizing as "bread straight from the oven".

This happened just when Tlaxcala was forced to surrender after a long siege against the Aztecs. What tribute could Tenochtitlan exact from so poor a city? The victors decreed that it be converted into a permanent battlefield for taking prisoner men destined to feed the Sun; and as Huitzilopochtli insisted that the captives offered to him must have fought bravely, the mutual hate between the two cities continued to be stirred up, probably even after a treaty of submission had already been signed.

Because of these wars, which went on till the arrival of the Spaniards, investigators tend to think that Tlaxcala remained independent of Tenochtitlan, a hypothesis difficult to support if the chronicles are carefully analysed. As the matter is important for an understanding of the mechanism of Aztec society, we quote in full a passage from the native historian, Ixtlilxochitl:

> ". . . Seeing that calamities did not cease, all met together with the nobles of Tlaxcala to discuss the most convenient method to achieve this. The priests and confessors of the Mexican temples said that the gods were wrathful against the empire, and that to appease them it would be well to

sacrifice many men. . . . Netzahualcoyotzin . . . said it was enough to sacrifice prisoners of war, who, having to die in battle, would lose little, moreover that it would be a great exploit for the soldiers to capture their enemies alive, with whom, besides being rewarded, they would make sacrifice to the gods; the priests replied that the wars they made were remote and infrequent, that the captives they must sacrifice to the gods would come in sparsely and very weak. . . . Xicotencatl, one of the nobles of Tlaxcala, thought that from that time forward it should be established that there would be wars between the nobles of Tlaxcala and Tezcuco, with their companies, and that a field should be marked out where these battles should generally be held, and that those who were taken prisoner and captive in them be sacrificed to their gods, which would be very acceptable to them, for as dainties they would be hot and fresh, taken from the field of battle; besides the fact that this would be the place where the sons of nobles should exercise, they would come away famous captains, and this, it should be understood, without exceeding the limits of the field so marked nor making any attempt to win lands and dominions, and likewise it must be with the qualification that when they had any trouble or crisis in one or other place they should cease these wars and help one another. . . . What Xicotencatl said was pleasing to all, and as they were interested and very religious . . . they hurried the business forward to put it into effect. . . ."[31]

As we see, these were no wars of independence but battles arranged by a perfectly legal pact. If, on the other hand, it is taken into account that the word Ixtlilxochitl puts into the mouths of the conquered Tlaxcaltecans were actually to be put into effect by the all-powerful Mexicans, it becomes clear that this pact, far from being an agreement between equals, represents a monstrous imposition.

The proofs of this are many, as for instance when we observe a king of Tenochtitlan or Tezcuco[32] giving orders to Tlaxcala chiefs, as is very neatly demonstrated in the following passages, which also give a vivid picture of the customs then obtaining on the plateau.

> "... The king (Netzahualcoyotl) when he saw that lady ... so beautiful and gifted with charm and natural talents ... stole her heart and, hiding his passion as well as he was able, took leave of the lord (husband to the lady) and went to his court, where he gave an order with all the secrecy in the world ... to send and deprive Quaquauhtzin of his life ... and it happened thus: he sent a message to the nobles of Tlaxcala ... saying that the death of Quaquauhtzin suited his kingdom ... and to give him an honourable death he asked the nobles to send their captains to kill him in battle, which should take place that day, in such a way that he should not return alive. ..."[33]

Some decades later, we see that Moctezuma II, intending to weaken the power of his ally, the king of Tezcoco, turns to Tlaxcala to perpetrate one of those betrayals of which the Aztec emperor was master:

> ". . . Moctezuma . . . secretly sent his ambassadors to the nobles of Tlaxcala advising them that the king of Tezcoco had gathered the most numerous and best of his armies, not for military exercises and sacrifice to the gods according to the law and custom established between them and protected by them and their leaders, but with intent to destroy and lay waste the province and dominion . . . this message caused great grief and pain in the dominion. . . ."[34]

And the same Moctezuma ordered that in the course of these battles among "friends of the house" (as he called the Tlaxcaltecans[35]), his brother, crown prince of Mexico, should be killed:

> "... According to general opinion, by the arrangement and secret pact the king Moctezuma had with the Tlaxcaltecans, on the pretext of avoiding disturbances and getting rid of anybody who stood in his way, he had his brother killed and overthrown in this battle, in which, together with him, died another Mexican noble named Tzicquaquatzin and two thousand eight hundred soldiers that went to his aid."[36]

It cannot always have been easy to keep the balance in so delicate a pact, since if the agreement had been known to the Tlaxcaltecan commoners the lives of their chiefs might have been threatened. Therefore when Aztec messengers arrived in Tlaxcala to invite the rulers of this "enemy" city to a feast, they accomplished their mission cunningly disguised and with the utmost secrecy. Only the wives of high-ranking nobles were allowed near the ambassadors, and these noble ladies served the meals and prepared their beds. Any indiscretion on the subject of these visits was punished with death. Muñoz Camargo, the historian of Tlaxcala, tells us that the Mexican nobles presented those of Tlaxcala with: "quantities of gold, cocoa, clothing, salt and all things they might need, without the common people knowing . . ."[37] and we see that at one particular ceremony the Tlaxcalan lords were treated by the king of Tenochtitlan with more consideration than any other of the chiefs of the imperial nations. The moving history of Tlalhuicole, hero of Tlaxcala, allows us to imagine some of the implications of such inhuman relations.

Tlalhuicole, an invincible general of the Tlaxcaltecan army, was captured one day by the Mexicans. The respect and admiration surrounding this soldier was so great that Moctezuma wished to take him into his service. Being a Tlaxcaltecan, he refused to serve his country's enemies, so the king then offered to return him to his people. Tlalhuicole would not accept his freedom and insisted on being sacrificed on the gladiator's stone, reserved for the bravest warriors. We are told that before dying, bound to the stone and with no more than a staff adorned with feathers, he killed eight warriors fully armed. Did this fearless man know that his country's chiefs were present at the combat disguised as Mexicans and hidden in a seat camouflaged with flowers? Did he know that after the particularly solemn ceremonies in his honour they were to eat amicably with the emperor of Tenochtitlan and were then to return to Tlaxcala laden with gifts? Had he known all this, would he have shown such heroism? Or was it precisely to put an end to a state of affairs he

8 KNIGHT EAGLE. Aztec sculpture in the Mexican National Museum

9 AZTEC DRUM. Mexican National Museum

considered infamous, that he rebelled against his chiefs' authority and threw himself into a desperate struggle against the Aztecs? This hypothesis, more plausible than the first, would explain both Moctezuma's attitude when he invited him to enter his services and the refusal of Tlalhuicole to return to his country, where he would have been condemned for insurrection.

Thus it seems evident that the Aztecs acted simply from political motives. To take their religious explanations of war seriously is to fall into a trap of State propaganda. Their lying formulae are shown up by one fact. The Aztec nobles were never themselves impatient to achieve the Solar glory in whose name they were slaughtering humanity. Their lust for life equalled their desire for power. If they had really believed that the one aim of existence was to give up their lives, sacrifice would not have been limited to supposedly inferior beings—slaves and prisoners—but would have been a privilege of the "elite". In fact everything points to the conclusion that the Aztec lords, although brought up in the doctrine of Quetzalcoatl, which taught men that inner perfection and spiritual sacrifice were supreme goals, had come to think of ritual slaughter only as a political necessity.

Thus two strong and opposed currents of thought existed in this society: on the one hand degenerate mysticism supporting an ambitious plan of conquest; on the other, Quetzalcoatl's doctrine as the one moral basis. So deep a contradiction must necessarily produce serious conflict. One of its earliest manifestations appeared toward the middle of the fifteenth century in the person of Netzahualcoyotl, king of Tezcoco, who in the name of an invisible god and creator, suddenly began to doubt the efficacy of human sacrifice.

Though it has sometimes been held that Netzahualcoyotl was the discoverer of a divine concept unknown until that time, it seems certain that he merely revived the concepts of the older faith. As the historian Alfredo Chavero astutely points out, ". . . the social milieu in which Netzahualcoyotl lived was not propitious to the development of such ideas. Moreover the Nahuas knew of the god creator and preserver of the universe."[38]

Ixtlilxochitl, who compiled his work with the help of ancient documents, in fact established the existence of a God creator at the very beginnings of Nahuatl history, many centuries before Netzahualcoyotl; and when we observe that in the Aztec prayers collected by Sahagún a deity "invisible and impalpable, like night and air" is frequently invoked, we are convinced that this concept had roots in the past and could not have been newly created.

Moreover there are a series of indications that allow us to suppose that Netzahualcoyotl was an adept in the religion of Quetzalcoatl, and it is surely not by chance that Ixtlilxochitl states: ". . . among the most serious leaders and keepers of history in these natives' ancient times, Quetzalcoatl is found to have been the first; and of the moderns, Netzahualcoyotl, king of Tezcoco."[39]

The relationship between the two is not at all surprising, for the same historian, tracing the origin of Tezcoco, several times mentions the special rôle of the Toltecs in the formation of that city. He tells how:

> ". . . when Quinatzin [first king of Tezcoco] had newly arrived in his empire, there came two nations from the Mixteca country . . . who were of Toltec lineage . . . skilled in the arts of painting and recording . . . [Quinatzin] made them settle in the city of Tezcoco."[40]

And later he adds:

> "Techotlalatzin [son of Quinatzin] entered into the succession to the empire . . . for his virtues . . . and because the nurse who raised him was a lady of the Toltec nation. . . . He was the first to use the Nahuatl tongue, now called Mexican, because his parents never used it; and thus he ordered the whole Chichimeca nation to speak it, particularly those that held office or duties . . . so that in it he preserved all the names of places, and good order . . . such as the use of painting and other matters of policy: which was easy for them because at that time they were very mixed with the Toltec nation. . . . The love in which Techotlalatzin

> held the Toltec nation was so great that he not only allowed them to live and settle among the Chichimecas, but also gave them facilities to make public sacrifice to the idols and dedicate their temples . . . and so from this time the Toltecs began to prevail in their rites and ceremonies."[41]

This was at about the time when the Aztecs were beginning to found their capital (1325). Nearly a hundred years later, in the time of Netzhualcoyotl, Tezcoco and Tenochtitlan were already holding:

> ". . . dominion and empire over all the rest, for the right they presumed to the whole land that had belonged to the Toltecs, whose successors and heirs they were. . . ."[42]

This formative century was crowded with fierce wars between the Chichimeca tribes for dominance over the Valley of Mexico.

When still a boy Netzahualcoyotl witnessed the assassination of his father, and to escape the enemies who had taken over the city of his forebears he lived a wretched, fugitive life until he was about thirty. No sooner had he reconquered his capital than he proceeded to beautify it. Ixtlilxochitl asserts that the great works he undertook were based on plans of ancient Tollan, and that it was thanks to the artistic talent of the Toltecs living there that Tezcoco became the centre of the arts and sciences in the Nahuatl world.

As his life shows, Netzahualcoyotl, though he seems to have been initiated into Quetzalcoatl's doctrine, was a man entirely identified with an epoch which possessed an unbridled desire for temporal power. Thus, though he built temples, gathered an incomparable library, and kept a brilliant court, we find him also waging cruel wars of conquest, supplying thousands of men to be sacrificed in Tenochtitlan, or intervening to impose a blood tribute on a conquered city.

But, precisely owing to his peculiar internal strength, this poet-king suffered because of his attempt to reconcile two irreconcilable concepts—on the one hand the idea that secular power was the aim of existence, on the other a nostalgia to reach beyond the human situation—and at one stage he attempted to fit his actions to the religion which he professed. This brief attempt, which does not appear to have in any way modified official customs, did however reveal what a marvellous power existed in a spiritual principle which the barbarians had believed they could betray with impunity. It is evident that Netzahualcoyotl did no more than give expression to a widespread attitude, an attitude that decided the history of the empire during the fifty remaining years of its life. It is said, for instance, that in the time of Netzahualcoyotl's son:

> "... on many nights there appeared a great splendour born in the east, climbing on high, and appearing in the form of a pyramid and with tongues of fire. ... They had news long since, and it was spoken of in their histories, that the times were now approaching in which the things Quetzalcoatl said and foretold would come to pass. ... And as the King of Tezcuco was so skilled in all the sciences they knew and had acquired, especially in astrology, in accord with the prophecies of their past ... he made little of his kingdom and domain and sent to the captains and leaders of his armies that they should stop the continuous wars they waged against Tlaxcala ... so that they should enjoy in all peace and tranquility the short time that remained to them of lordship and command ..."[43]

In the person of Moctezuma II, the emperor who received Cortés and died ingloriously, hit by a stone, we can better follow the extraordinary process of disintegration of the Aztec empire.

Incarnation of Sun and State, Moctezuma was undisputed master of a world so perfectly organized that the individual was no more than a mechanism. The system seemed established for eternity, and no one dared defy the ruling philosophy unless he was at the same time prepared to place himself on the fringes of society. The legal texts condemning to capital punishment those who refused to witness a human sacrifice were doubtless by now already purely formal, for any individual rebellion was considered a case of dementia rather than of lawlessness.

Coming to power at the apotheosis of the Aztec tribe, Moctezuma was raised to a dizzy height: his person was sacred, his despotism limitless. In spite of this it appears, from what we know of his life, that a deep anguish ruled this sovereign of a state apparently solid as rock.

Moctezuma's reign was in fact marked by the appearance of innumerable signs foretelling the end of the Empire. These disturbing auguries, which all the chroniclers speak of and no historian has doubted, were observed over a period of seventeen years and were clear signs of a serious inner crisis in the Aztec world. In these auguries Moctezuma was always singled out as being responsible for the catastrophes that were to come; and, oddly enough, this terrible despot, instead of showing anger, underwent long penances for his salvation.

Why this feeling that he was to blame? Now that the State was well-founded he might have allowed himself to moderate his violence; whereas, in order to construct this vast empire, his predecessors had had to act as fiercely toward their own people as towards those they ruled. Aztec history is pervaded by murder, betrayal, and blood-curdling sacrifices, but there is never any sign of remorse toward the victims.

Why did Moctezuma allow criticism and admit himself to blame for the errors he committed because his wise men read messages into the passage of a comet? Why this desperate need to justify, and this panic which he suffered throughout his reign? How can we explain the anguish of this all-powerful sovereign, except by a crack in the political philosophy which ought to have upheld him?

Clearly Moctezuma was the representative of a system founded upon beliefs which were now being thrown into doubt. As doubt spread, so he was obliged to adopt an authoritarian attitude; because for him, as for every tyrant, doubt is synonymous with death. For many years he was to vacillate between the old, resurgent spirituality, and the destructive concepts propping up his empire. It was this struggle against a faith in which he had been brought up that gave birth to his feeling of guilt.

He tried to avoid it, first by unsuccessful flight, and then by death. But he was always forced inexorably to return to his post as executioner and victim. Maddened by this rôle and, despairing lest he might never free himself from it, he took up contradictory attitudes and we hear of him alternating between prolonged fasts and cruel reprisals against those whose lack of orthodoxy was undermining the empire.

The testimonies to the power of this conflict are many. Here is an example:

> ". . . In that year Moctezuma killed Tzompantecuctli of Cuitláhuac and all his sons. The murderers were the Cuitlahuacas themselves, by order of Moctezuma, King of Mexico. Tzompantecuctli's answer to Moctezuma was the cause of his death. He [Moctezuma] had asked Tzompantecuctli's advice about what to do; he had said, 'It had seemed to me fitting that Huitzilopochtli's house should be of massive gold, and that within it should be of emerald and rich *quetzalli* plumes. Thus will the tribute of the world be exacted; for our god has need of it. What thinkest thou?' Tzompantecuctli answered and said: 'Our king and master, it is not thus. Understand that with this shalt thou hasten the ruin of thy people and thou shalt offend the heaven we see above. Understand our god shall not be the one who is now; he is coming who shall become lord over all and maker of all creatures.' Hearing this, Moctezuma waxed wrathful and told Tzompantecuctli, 'Go, and may thy words stick in thy throat.' So died Tzompantecuctli and all his sons."[44]

This could not be more explicit. The allusions to the end of the Aztec kingdom, to its usurping god, and to the coming of a "lord over all" indicate clearly that there was a struggle going on between opposed concepts. Moreover it is well known that the "maker of all creatures" was none other than Quetzalcoatl, just as history also tells us that in the person of Cortés Moctezuma saw the very god who would return to assume power once more.

In addition there exists the testimony of the auguries which, fantastic as they appear, do nevertheless indicate an open crisis, for so many heralding signs could only arise in a world that had lost its equilibrium.

There were inextinguishable fires; comets traversing the sky for hours on end; the enchanted crane bearing the mirror in which a starry sky appeared in the middle of the day; the strange tale of the shepherd borne by an eagle to a shining grotto where he was received by a person "compared with whom Moctezuma was nothing"; and many other sure indications of the downfall of the Empire.

Preferring to end things once for all, Moctezuma decided to die, and he sent emissaries laden with sumptuous gifts—skins of flayed men—to the Lord of the Land of the Dead. But Huemac refused to take the king into his service (he had asked to enter as dustman), and when the ambassadors returned with the bad news they were killed.

Other messengers, laden like their predecessors with skins of flayed men, set off on this dangerous expedition. Huemac then made it known to Moctezuma that his case had been lost through bad conduct, "through his great pride and cruelty to his kin," and deep purification was recommended. Moctezuma willingly submitted to a fast of twenty-four days.

This penance being without result, he made a last attempt at evasion and hid on a small island. One of his ministers became aware of his flight and, giving him moral advice and promising to say nothing if he conducted himself as he should, made him return shamefaced to his palace.

Boundless panic now seized Moctezuma. Cost what it might, he was determined to discover "that which must come".

He gathered all the court sorcerers and besought them to reveal the dreadful secret. As their replies were unsatisfactory, they were all put to death. . . .

The astrologers were accused of treason because they had been unable to read anything in the signs of the sky; and they were killed. . . .

Anyone dreaming anything about the end of the Empire was ordered to the palace to tell of it. Night and day emissaries combed the city, and Tenochtitlan paid tribute in dreams. . . . But finding no good in the thousands offered, Moctezuma killed all the offenders. It was the massacre of the dreamers, the most pathetic of all. . . .

From that day there were no more forecasts, no more dreams. Terror weighed upon the spirit world, and Moctezuma remained alone with his unspeakable anguish.

He could not bear this crushing silence. He longed for reassuring voices.

Soldiers went to the most distant regions to bring wise men, by force if need be, to replace those who had been exterminated. These strangers declared that "very soon what must come would come"; but when the king wanted to know more, some witchcraft caused them prudently to disappear.

At last one day there arrived at the palace a man who told that he had seen "a mountain that went from side to side of the sea without ever touching the coasts". Moctezuma had the man thrown into prison and sent his emissaries to verify his statements.

When his messengers returned with an exact description of what they had seen, the king remained "with his head cast down, uttering no word".

For the first time in many years Moctezuma could breathe freely: uncertainty and fear had ended. Faced with this concrete danger, his spirit revived; he gave orders, and formulated plans. Anything is better than doubt, and it is easy to believe Cortés when he describes to the king of Spain how Moctezuma, during all the time he was his prisoner, wore "a happy face".

Moctezuma received the Spanish captain on his arrival in Tenochtitlan, saying:

> ". . . Many days, through our scriptures, have we news that neither I nor any living in this land are natives of it, but strangers come to it from very distant parts; and likewise we know that a lord whose vassals they all are, who returned to his native land, brought this generation to these parts. . . .

> And we have always known that those from whom they descended must come to rule this land and ourselves as its vassals. And according to the place you say you come from, from whence the sun rises, and the things you say of this great lord or king that sent you here, we believe and hold him verily to be our true lord; especially since you say that he has had news of us many days. And therefore be you certain that we shall obey you and hold you lord in place of this great lord you speak of and in whom there is no fault or deceit whatever: and well may you in all the land, I say in those domains I possess, order according to your will, for you shall be obeyed and acted upon, and all we have is for you to dispose of as you please. . . ."[45]

His later behaviour in no way belied these words, and can be understood only in their light. It is otherwise impossible to explain how this despot not only accepted without sorrow or rebellion his capture in the midst of his own guards, the plundering of his palace, the bad manners of the Spanish soldiers—manners that deeply shocked his refined tastes—but how he also intervened on behalf of the aggressors when the whole city rose in rebellion because of the slaughter in the patio of the Great Temple. He died from a stone thrown in revenge against him when he was trying to calm his subjects from high up on the terrace.

IX

CAUSES OF THE FALL OF THE AZTEC EMPIRE

To understand why the Spanish conquest was so easy it is necessary above all to remember that the Empire was deeply undermined by many conflicts, those of a religious and political nature being the most disturbing. The spiritual ferment caused by the rebirth of Quetzalcoatl's tradition, besides encouraging a will to independence, must also have been stimulated by it. We have proof of this in the history of the assassination of Tzompantecutli, chief of a conquered territory which, in the name of religious principles, refused to pay the higher tribute—gold and ade—which Moctezuma proposed on the pretext that it was divinely necessary.

Moreover the "conquest" was no more than a series of rebellions on the part of the vassal states, who were clearly only waiting the most propitious moment to shake off the Aztec yoke. We read that the inhabitants of a town neighbouring on Tenochtitlan—Xochimilco by name—were accused of espionage and slaughtered to the last man. The treason of the chiefs of the conquered provinces in favour of the Spaniards, who promised to help them break loose from Mexican dominion, is eloquent proof that in the whole land there existed only hate for the oppressors. Nothing else explains the Spanish victories: to wonder, as is frequently done, at the exploits of a handful of invaders, is simply to forget that these were promptly supported by tens of thousands of native warriors.

This hostility toward the Aztecs seems to show that the belief in a holy war which the latter so freely propagated has been taken more seriously by modern students than by the Meso-american peoples themselves. If faith in the general cosmic need for ritual killing had existed, these betrayals would have been unthinkable, the more so since, as archaeology has proved, the Nahuatl religion was firmly rooted throughout Mexico.

So the sacred nature of the Aztec state in no way facilitated the conquest. That it could have done so is impossible to believe if we remember the way the Aztecs behaved throughout their sojourn on the plateau. In fact exactly the contrary might be suspected, that it was precisely the Aztecs desire for temporal power that caused their downfall. It is certain, for instance, that the lack of solidarity in the provinces could have arisen only out of resentment provoked by the Aztecs' excessive rapacity, and the hateful way in which they distorted a deeply revered religious tradition. It is probable that if the Meso-american people—whose deep religious feeling cannot be doubted—had regarded Tenochtitlan as a real spiritual power, events would have taken a very different course.

Moctezuma's passiveness was in all probability due to his following the law of least resistance. It is possible that, enfeebled by his own abuses of power and the threats he had for many years felt rising round him, this strange figure seized the opportunity offered him to escape the weight of imperial direction. Faith in Quetzalcoatl's return—which he did not for long identify with the arrival of Cortés—must have served as a suitable excuse for what his own conscience knew was a sacriligeous desertion.

Whatever the truth about Moctezuma, Tenochtitlan's desperate resistance, and also Cuauhtémoc's heroism when he faced his Spanish executioners[46], clearly show that Aztec society possessed enormous reserves of strength which might one day have been directed toward a less destructive ideal than that which their nomad, hunting past had bequeathed to them. In any case it is not impossible to suppose that the contradictions at that time undermining Mexico might have resolved themselves in some formula favourable to mankind. The very existence of such conflicts in the midst of so dreadful a tyranny forces us to recognize a vitality rich in promise.

It remains only to ask: how would Aztec society have evolved if it had been granted a few more centuries of life? All that can be said is that a return of Quetzalcoatl's reign in the pure form in which it had been known in Tollan would have been impossible after the Chichimecas had arrived and established themselves on the plateau. After the tenth century the Precolumbian world was turned upside down by concepts till then unknown: that the kingdom of earth was more important than the kingdom of heaven; that social man must be the centre of all aspiration; that the deity intervened only in order to support purely terrestrial aims. For three or four centuries even the gods were openly supplanted by warrior concepts and organizations.[47] It was not until the middle of the fifteenth century that these gods acquired new strength, and then it was in the service of a cruel state philosophy.

We may perhaps idly imagine that, with inspired mysticism

as a basis, and with the elementary determinism and unbridled will toward material conquest of the Chichimecas superseded, the Meso-american people might, thanks to their prodigious creative power, have succeeded in forging a synthesis of human and divine such as that which Greece was once able to offer the West.

NOTES

1. Fr. Bernardino de Sahagún, *Historia General de las Cosas de Nueva España*, Editorial Nueva España, S.A., Mexico, 1946, Vol. III, p. 47.
2. Sahagún, op. cit., vol. III, p. 85.
3. Angel María Garibay, *Historia de la Literatura Nahuatl*, Editorial Porrua, S.A., Mexico, 1953, pp. 472-3. The year "3-House" and the sign "1-Snake" refer to the Aztec system of calculating time.
4. *Ibid.*, p. 477.
5. Bernal Díaz del Castillo, *Historia Verdadera de la Conquista de Nueva España*, Ediciones Mexicanas S.A., Mexico, 1950, p. 164.
6. *Ibid.*, p. 178.
7. Hernán Cortés, *Cartas de Relación de la Conquista de México*. Espasa Calpe, Argentina S.A., 1945, pp. 87-91.
8. *Ibid.*, p. 92.
9. Translated from the Nahuatl into Spanish by Angel María Garibay, op. cit., pp. 148, 176.
10. Sahagún, op. cit., Vol. I, pp. 639, 530.
11. *Ibid.*, p. 605.
12. *Ibid.*, pp. 472-7.
13. *Ibid.*, Vol. II, pp. 142, 143, 152.
14. Bernal Díaz del Castillo, op. cit., p. 179.
15. Sahagún, op. cit., Vol. I, pp. 97, 99, 100, 101, 102, 105.
16. *Ibid.*, p. 135.
17. Wigberto Jiménez Moreno, *Fray Bernardino de Sahagún y Su Obra*, Editorial Pedro Robredo, México, 1938, pp. 7, 8.
18. *Codice Ramírez*, Editorial Leyenda, Mexico, 1944, p. 24.
19. Tezozomoc, *Cronica Mexicana*, Imprenta Ireneo Paz, Mexico, 1878, p. 10.
20. *Ibid.*, p. 13.

21. Sahagún, op. cit., Vol. II, p. 275.
22. *Ibid.*, pp. 276, 278, 279, 280, 281.
23. *Ibid.*, p. 278.
24. Fernando de Alva Ixtlilxochitl, *Obras Históricas,* Secretaria de Fomento, Mexico, 1892, Vol. II, p. 318.
25. Sahagún, op. cit., Vol. II, p. 35.
26. H. J. Spinden, *New Light on Quetzalcoatl*, Congreso Internacional de Americanistas, Paris, 1947.
27. Alfonso Caso, *El Pueblo del Sol,* Fondo de Cultura Económica, Mexico, 1953, p. 40.
28. Sahagún, op. cit., Vol. I, p. 330.
29. *Ibid.*, pp. 136-7.
30. *Ibid.*, pp. 192-3.
31. *Obras Historicas de Don Fernando de Alva Ixtlilxochitl, Mexico,* 1892, Vol. II, pp. 206-7.
32. Besides Tenochtitlan, there existed on the plateau various cities, Tezcoco being the most important.
33. Fernando Ixtlilxochitl, op. cit., Vol. II, pp. 214-5.
34. *Ibid.*, pp. 214-5.
35. *Ibid.*, p. 207.
36. *Ibid.*, pp. 309-10.
37. Diego Muñoz Camargo, *Historia de Tlaxcala*, Mexico, 1944, p. 124.
38. Note by Chavero on p. 255 of Ixtlilxochitl, op. cit.
39. Ixtlilxochitl, op. cit., Vol. II, p. 21.
40. *Ibid.*, p. 21.
41. *Ibid.*, p. 70.
42. *Ibid.*, p. 190.
43. *Ibid.*, pp. 313-4.
44. *Anales de Cuauhtitlan*, Imprenta Universitaria, Mexico, 1945, p. 61.
45. Hernán Cortés, op. cit., p. 70.
46. Cuauhtémoc—a Nahuatl name meaning "Falling Eagle"—was the last Aztec Emperor. He commanded the siege of Tenochtitlan and was later hanged by Cortés in the heart of the tropical forest of Chiapas.
47. This period of cultural transition is discernable in certain archaeological cities of a purely secular character, as, among others, Tula-Xicotitlan in the state of Hidalgo, perhaps the most representative of this moment of frank power politics (1100-1300).

PART II

The Nahuatl Religion

I

MAGIC

SPEAKING GENERALLY, we may roughly distinguish three main phases in the development of human culture in its advance from primitive beginnings to greater awareness: first the magical, then the religious, and lastly the historical.*

Although these main stages can be detected in the rise of most civilizations, it is probable that in none are they so clearly distinguishable as in ancient Mexico.

Throughout Mexico archaeology has recognized an archaic period of roughly three thousand years, extending up to about the beginnings of the Christian era—during which men lived in small agricultural communities, made ceramics sometimes of great beauty, and buried their dead with offerings. No god, no transcendental symbol, appears during these centuries, which are ruled entirely by magic.

We shall try to define this magic as clearly as possible in order to discover the elements that made it irreconcilable with the

* In writing this section of the book I am aware that my division may meet opposition, but I am more and more convinced that the religious and the magical phases of a culture are distinct and unrelated. If we try to understand as humbly as possible what actually existed, we see that in the archaeological material of the early period the divinity is non-existent. What I am trying to discover is how men thought who appear to have known nothing about God because they did not represent the deity in any form, and who therefore looked upon the universe quite differently from other men who have left evidence that they understood the idea of divinity. Unfortunately in this book I have not been able to discuss the matter fully. I hope to do so in a later study.

religion which follows and which is the main theme of this study.

The period dominated by magic seems not to have been very sympathetically investigated by the rationalists, who have neglected to study the kind of thinking which led to it and have limited themselves to examining the end-results of magical practices. Thus Frazer, the most important representative of this school, arrives at a definition of magic apparently determined entirely by the type of scientific thought current during his own epoch. Had he not held that the desire to act upon external nature was an end in itself, he might never have arrived at the concept that the beliefs of primitive man were ruled by rudimentary scientific notions. For though it is quite probable that the history of disciplined observation dates back to these distant ages, this fact explains nothing at all about the inner attitude of archaic man.

The error seems to exist in assuming science to have evolved out of magic and religion, when in fact it is an entirely different phenomenon. The problem of domination over the external world is thus confused with the philosophical problem of existence, a problem which is foreign to science. If our knowledge of magical and religious thought in the Pre-columbian world is not to be hopelessly vague, we must try to understand the concepts of life such modes of thought imply.

If we study contemporary works referring to archaic peoples, we become convinced that the chief characteristic of a cultural state dominated by magic is that the human being appears quite unreal. Still incapable of synthesis, man finds himself unprotected in a world without a centre, and he sees in every one of its manifestations a separate, individual will, which is imposed upon him and which he can subdue only by identification with it. The sorcerer, supreme representative of this attitude, appears to possess the power to *live* things, to identify himself with them. If he invokes rain by imitating rain it is not, as in modern technology, because he believes he can know the laws that will unfailingly produce it. He himself becomes rain, and once this metamorphosis is achieved the rain is already there in his person. Only if the metamorphosis is incomplete does the operation fail. So, entirely convinced, he is himself the bear that lets itself be trapped, the illness that escapes from the body that holds it, the full ear of maize that is desired, the huge fish falling into the net; all, in fact, that is needed for the community. This naturally implies previous observation of phenomena, but faith in the efficacy of the imitation lies in something other than a mechanical view of the universe.

Study of the archaeological material from the archaic Precolumbian period, composed mainly of naturalistic representations of animals and women, will help to make this clear. The former are easily explained. The custom of modelling images of animals the people needed in abundance is not only mentioned in ancient documents but has been observed by many modern ethnologists. The female figures, on the other hand, have been so argued about that the understanding of this magical phase becomes more and more difficult. If, as some have suggested, these female images represent an earth goddess, it means that the concept of divinity enters history several centuries earlier than it theoretically should; for archaeological collections show that this advanced concept closes the archaic period and is always accompanied by a number of cultural characteristics entirely lacking in earlier times.

Moreover ethnology seems to show clearly enough that the fundamental psychological attitude of primitive man is to assimilate the multitudinous forms of nature to himself. Such assimilation contradicts the principle of singularity or wholeness inherent in the idea of divinity. The American anthropologist, Clew Parsons, tells how the Pueblo Indians speak familiarly of girls as "white maize", "yellow maize", "red maize", and adds that young virgins take the parts of these important crops, impersonating them in certain ceremonies. These symbolic representations form the theme of many tales of the Zapotec Indians from southern Mexico:

10 ROUND TEMPLE of the Knights Eagle and Tiger at Malinalco

11 INTERIOR OF THE TEMPLE at Malinalco

12 MAYAN SCULPTURED STONE, discovered in Palenque in 1953

"A man met a boy and a girl at the cross. 'I am Corn,' said the boy, 'and she is Beans.' That year they had five crops at Mitla."

And again:

"Lightning brought out two flower vases and from them came out two girls, one girl had no colour . . . the other was red and very attractive. Then he said to Pablo: 'Now which of these girls will you take? Here you have the crops.' "[1]

Tales of this kind are valuable because, besides showing that the custom of personifying natural phenomena persists to our day, they allow us better to understand the mechanism of the magic rite: the apparition of the girl maize or bean has such splendid consequences that every effort is made to encourage it. That is, the magical activity consists in performing pantomimes in which human beings assume the rôles of animals, plants, and clouds, which are thus conjured up and enacted according to the needs of the group. It is, then, legitimate to suppose that the female archaic images represent the good things needed by the Indians in abundance, a hypothesis that seems to be confirmed by the most significant relevant material from any Pre-Columbian archaic centre, that found in Tlatilco, a suburb of Mexico City.

Owing to its perfect cultural integration and the fact that its date (1500 B.C.) has been fairly accurately established, Tlatilco is like a beacon on the road of prehistory. From its unique position it throws light both on the dark periods before it and on the equally dark ones that follow. Here in Tlatilco certain more evolved ways of life—the beginnings of a social structure, division of labour, collective participation in ritual—become manifest for the first time in Meso-america, and it was perhaps these new forms that helped the inhabitants to attain an artistic expression infinitely superior to that of their predecessors or immediate followers.

The objects from Tlatilco are full of unusual spontaneity. Among the ceramic objects—sometimes brilliantly free in invention—there is an extraordinary number of figurines. Representations of men—almost always oddities—dwarfs, hunchbacks, magicians—form a tiny percentage of the whole. The female figures are surprising in their quantity as well as their seductive quality. They are of all ages, and appear in the most unexpected poses, but most of them are of the type called by archaeologists "the pretty woman", because they represent such charming ladies, extremely beautiful and elegant. Usually naked, they are always adorned with jewels and coiffures, the variety and sophisticated forms of which remind one of women dressed up for solemn feasts. In spite of the diversity of expression and adornment, they have nearly always certain characteristics in common: childlike faces, adolescent bodies covered with paint (usually yellow, occasionally white, black, or purple), with hair and extremities painted red.

These special characteristics seem to indicate that the figurines represented tender ears of maize. Everything suggests this: their virginity—ethnographic documents always point out that only virgins took part in the rituals in honour of this cereal; the colours of the body—yellow, red, white, or purple as the grains themselves; and the hair, long and red as the maize beard. In the description given by Sahagún of the Aztec ceremonies in honour of maize—about three thousand years after Tlatilco—we find young dancers adorned in precisely the same manner as these figurines.

There also exist double images of this same childlike person. Basing our argument on the happy significance the primitive peoples of the American continent usually assign to twins, we have elsewhere suggested[2] that these attractive pieces must represent double ears of corn.

Remembering the importance of maize for American peoples, we can easily believe that most of the "pretty women" of Tlatilco represented this cereal. Recent works on this subject mention the figurines, which are made either of clay or wood, rags or maize leaves, which personify sometimes the last ear found in the field after gathering, sometimes the mother of the maize enclosed in the granary to guard the harvest, or sometimes the bride or groom of the maize. . . .

Be this as it may, it seems probable that these archaic figures are simple images of actual things and have no more complex significance. It is interesting to observe that, in spite of their undeniable creative power, the artists of Tlatilco do not even begin to approach the religious ideas which later predominated in Meso-america. Though they sometimes achieve surprising stylization, their works never show the symbolic attributes which are the one and only testimony of a capacity for synthesis, without which the deity cannot exist. Moreover, archaeological documents prove that after Tlatilco many centuries went by—until the beginning of our era—before the first god made his appearance.

II

RELIGION AND THE QUETZALCOATL MYTH

In the evolution of thought, the archaic seems to represent the pre-religious stage, before any principle appears to bind phenomena together; from which we deduce that the world of magic is essentially one of multiplicity and fragmentation, in which every component part is an isolated entity having no inner communion with the rest. Religion, on the other hand, conceiving the various parts to be emanations from an invisible whole, puts an end to such a state of division: herein lies its transcendence.

The principle of wholeness inherent in religion—a principle having very little to do with the quality and number of the gods—signifies that man has discovered a centre in himself and that he thinks of the universe as radiating from this centre. That is, the true essence of every religious system lies in the revelation of an individual soul closely bound to the soul of the cosmos: it has to do, in other words, with making man divine. Being merely perishable products of the intellect swayed by social circumstance, the gods are secondary and, considered as an end in themselves, can lead only to error. Thus if we wish to arrive at the essential elements of a religion, we must bypass inert technical details and make an effort to rediscover the revelation existing inevitably at its source.

As to the Nahuatl religion, this primordial revelation is expressed with great density and luminosity in the different myths of Quetzalcoatl, myths which fill most of the documents of Meso-american history.

The first of these refers to Quetzalcoatl as a king wholly chaste until the day on which, under pressure from evil counsellors, he gets drunk and commits a carnal act. In despair at what he considers to be the most horrible of sins, he decides to punish himself as an example: he abandons his beloved kingdom and dies voluntarily by fire. His body burns, and his heart rises to heaven where it is transformed into the planet Venus.

In a desperate effort to preserve something concrete from the vague mass of Pre-columbian history, some investigators have tried to reduce this first myth to fact, attaching it to events in the life of a tenth-century warrior possessed of a cut-and-dried biography. Apart from the fact that technically there is no foundation for making such an identification, it seems doubtful whether one man's drunkenness could ever be converted into the central theme of the history of a people. It would be possible to explain only a small part of Quetzalcoatl's existence in terms of human biography; episodes such as his transformation into the planet Venus and his descent into the Land of the Dead are closely allied to, and just as important as, the story of his drunkenness. Everything indicates, in fact, that we are in the presence of a true myth. To wish to convert it into a fragment of history is to destroy it and deprive it forever of its vital content; because the myth, the most profound expression of the spirit, oversteps the boundaries of particular detail and always achieves the revelation of a fundamental, eternal truth.

The spiritual content of the Quetzalcoatl myth is self-evident: the anguish for his sin, his burning need for purification, and also the fire that converts him into light, reveal a religious doctrine closely related to those humanity has known elsewhere under various symbolic languages.

In fact it appears to speak of the beginnings of an individual soul, which can attain to a superior, liberating consciousness through painful human experience in which sin—the dark side of corporeal life—is as necessary as the bright side.

The Meso-american peoples have pointed out the transcendence of this message. In most of their myths of creation, for instance, it is said that during the four eras previously destroyed the earth was populated only by animals, and it was not until the advent of the Era of Quetzalcoatl that humanity was created. This suggests that it is only after the discovery of the spiritual principle as lived by Quetzalcoatl that man could *be.* This is doubtless the reason why Quetzalcoatl was considered as creator of the human being and all his works.

Fully to appreciate the importance of this revelation, it must be remembered that in the archaic epochs out of which this great bringer of civilization arose, the individual as such did not exist. Immersed in the mists of magic, man represented little more than a mechanism to register wills outside his control, until Quetzalcoatl—the magician *par excellence,* "he who knows the secret of all enchantments," at last initiated him into the mysteries of the interior life, thus freeing him from the unprotected solitude of pre-individual existence.

Belief in the spiritual principle appears to be the very basis of the Nahuatl religion. All Aztec testimonies clearly show man to be the incarnation of a celestial particle. Here, for example, are the words in which a Tenochtitlan father announces his daughter's pregnancy:

> "Know then all of you that our lord has had mercy, for the Lady N., a young maiden recently married, has within her a precious stone and a rich feather, since the young woman is now pregnant . . ."[3]

And here are the midwife's words to the newborn:

> "My well loved and tender son . . . know and understand

that thy house is not here . . . This house wherein thou art born is but a nest, an inn at which thou hast arrived, thy entry into this world: here dost thou bud and flower . . . thy true house is another."[4]

And again:

"Oh precious stone, oh rich feather . . . thou wert made in the place where are the great God and Goddess which are above the heavens[5]. . . Thy mother and thy father, celestial woman and celestial man, made and reared thee. . . . Thou hast come to this world from afar, poor and weary. . . . Our Lord Quetzalcoatl, who is the creator, has put into this dust a precious stone and a rich feather."[6]

There are many indications that the human soul was represented symbolically by the precious stone or feather. Two of the most interesting examples of the use of this symbology occur in the lives of Quetzalcoatl and of Huitzilopochtli. In the Annals of Cuauhtitlán we read: ". . . it is said that the mother of Quetzalcoatl conceived because she swallowed an emerald stone."[7] Huitzilopochtli's mother found herself pregnant after having in her bosom a white feather she had found while sweeping the temple. It would therefore seem that, as in the Christian mystery of the Incarnation, the spirit falls from on high to penetrate the body of a woman.

The myth also suggests the heavenly origin of man. It is significant that the demons who decide, because of Quetzalcoatl's irritating purity, to cause his downfall, invent exactly the trick of "giving him his body". Let us see how the Annals of Cuauhtitlán have recorded this robust parable of human destiny:

". . . Those who called themselves Tezcatlipoca, Ihuimécatl and Toltécatl said, 'He must leave his village, where we intend to live.' And added: 'Let us make pulque; we shall give it him to drink so that he loses his skill and has no more power.' "

Then Tezcatlipoca spoke: 'I say that we should give him his body.'

How shall we tell how they contrived mutually to bring it about!

First came Tezcatlipoca; he took a double mirror the size of a hand's span and wrapped it up; when he came to where Quetzalcoatl was, he said to the acolytes that guarded him: 'Go and say to the priest: a youth has come to show thee thy body, Lord, and to give it thee.'

The acolytes entered and informed Quetzalcoatl, who said to them: 'What is this . . . ? What thing is my body? Look and see what he has brought and then he may enter.'

He [Tezcatlipoca] did not wish to let them see it and said: 'Go and say to the priest that I myself must show it to him.'

They went and told him: 'He does not agree; he insists on showing it to thee, Lord.'

Quetzalcoatl said: 'Enter, grandfather.'

They went to call Tezcatlipoca; he entered, greeted him, and said: 'Son of mine, Priest Ce Acatl Quetzalcoatl, I greet thee and come, Lord, to show thee thy body.'

Quetzalcoatl said: 'I know and welcome thee, grandfather. Whence hast thou come? What is this concerning my body? Let us see.'

Then he gave him the mirror and said: 'Look and know thyself my son, for thou shalt appear in the mirror.'

Then Quetzalcoatl saw himself; he was very frightened and said: 'If my vassals were to see me, they might run away.' "

Instigated by the demons, he gets drunk and then sleeps with the lovely Quetzalpetatl. But:

". . . At dawn they were saddened and his heart softened. Then said Quetzalcoatl: 'Woe is me!'

And he sang the sad song he had made that he might depart thence: 'This is an evil tale of a day when I left my house. May those that are absent be softened, it was hard and perilous for me. Only let the one whose body is of earth exist and sing; I did not grow up subjected to servile labour.'

When Quetzalcoatl sang, all his acolytes were sad and

wept. Then they also sang: 'In an alien house my lords have not yet grown rich. Quetzalcoatl has no headdress of precious stones. Perhaps somewhere the timbers are clean. Behold him here. Let us weep.'

When his acolytes had sung, Quetzalcoatl said to them: 'Acolytes, it is enough. I shall leave the village, I shall go away. Order a stone box to be made.'

At once they made a box of stone. And when it was finished, there lay Quetzalcoatl. Four days only he was in the stone box. When he began to feel unwell he said to his acolytes: 'Acolytes, it is enough, let me go. Seal it well and hide the riches and good things we have found and all our possessions . . .'

At once went Quetzalcoatl; he stood; he called his pages and wept with them. Then they went to Tlillan Tlapallan, the burner. . . .

It is said that . . . having reached the celestial shore of the divine water (the seacoast), he stopped, cried, seized his garments, and put on his insignia of feathers and his green mask. . . . Then when he was adorned he set fire to himself and burned. . . . It is said that when he burned his ashes were at once raised up and that all the rare birds appeared when Quetzalcoatl died, for which reason they call him Lord of Dawn. They say that when he died dawn did not appear for four days, because he had gone to dwell among the dead; and that in four days he provided himself with arrows; for which reason in eight days there appeared the great star called Quetzalcoatl. And they add that he was enthroned as Lord."[8]

It is impossible not to feel the hermetic quality of this tale, which, because of its deep poetic inspiration, can be numbered among the most beautiful texts of the great religious traditions.

So in the parable it is Venus whom Quetzalcoatl chooses to represent the soul; this planet is thus situated at the centre of the cosmic drama in which man will presently play one of the chief rôles.

After first appearing in the western sky,[9] Venus disappears "underground" and remains hidden for several days, reappearing, brighter than ever, in the eastern sky when she reunites with the sun. The soul follows the same route: she descends from her celestial home and enters the darkness of matter, only to rise again, glorious, at the moment of the body's dissolution. The myth of Quetzalcoatl signifies just this. The King's absolute purity refers to the state of the planet when it is still nothing but light. His sins and remorse correspond to the phenomenon of the incarnation of this light and the painful but necessary assumption of human form; his abandonment of the things of this world, and the fatal fire he builds with his own hands, show the precepts which have to be followed if human existence is not to be lost: the attainment of eternal unity through detachment from, and sacrifice of, the transitory self.

A page of the Codex Borbonicus contains an iconographic document showing the same relationsip between Venus and the soul: there is a picture of a dead warrior surrounded by ritual objects; among these his mask is significant, since it is the mask of the Morning Star in its human form, clearly showing that the soul of the warrior represents the planet on its way to unite with the sun.

The same thought is expressed in the following quotation:

> "... I pray Your Majesty, our most human Lord ... that thou shalt think it fitting that those who died in this war be received with feelings of purity and love by our father the Sun."[10]

For the Aztecs death in battle was the supreme purification, and this priest prays that the sun may hold the spirit of the dead worthy to be gathered back to heaven. It is in this sense that the deity needs human help. Owing to the fact that it detaches a little from itself in every creature, it would end by dying if the individual, leading a life of darkness and unconsciousness, were to destroy the particle he had received instead of returning it still brighter than before.

That is, creation is held to be impossible except through sacrifice: the sacrifice of the Sun dismembered among human kind (the Evening Star—spirit before incarnation—was a fragment of light torn off before its decline); the sacrifice of men to restore the sun's original unity.

In another passage relating to the same myth—which Sahagún has fortunately preserved—it is easy to see the relationship that exists between the human soul, represented by Venus, and the Sun. It is said that once Quetzalcoatl had set out on his pilgrimage to the east—a pilgrimage which must certainly represent the planet's "underground" passage back to the sun—a number of:

> ". . . necromancers came to meet him to stop him from advancing further, saying to Quetzalcoatl: 'Whither goest thou? Why hast thou left thy people? To whom dost thou commend thyself? Who will do penance?' And Quetzalcoatl answering these necromancers, said unto them, 'There is no way in which you can stop my departure, for I must go'; and the necromancers asked Quetzalcoatl once again 'Whither goes thou?' And he answered, saying: 'I go to Tlapallan.' 'Why goest thou?' asked the necromancers. And he replied, 'They have come to call me, the Sun is calling me.' To which they made answer: 'Go, and fare well.' "[11]

But the document that throws most light on this point is that referring to the communion it was usual to make once a year with Huitzilopochtli, sun god above all. In case it should be thought of as merely one ritual among many, we quote the passage in which Sahagún speaks of the conditions the Priests of Tenochtitlan thought necessary to impose upon those participating in the ceremonies:

> "The youths who were to receive Huitzilopochtli's body were obliged to serve one year . . . and together with the youths, the ministers of the other gods . . . did great service and penitence from which they suffered more weakness and exhaustion than they could bear . . . when the year was over they celebrated the feast in honour of Huitzilopochtli . . . They took seeds of grain and cleaned them well . . . they

ground them carefully, then when the flour was very fine they made dough and with this modelled the body of Huitzilopochtli. Next day a man named Quetzalcoatl shot the body of Huitzilopochtli with an arrow having a stone head, and thrust it into his heart . . . and after having killed him, they broke him in pieces . . . and they took Huitzilopochtli's heart to the lord or King, and all the body and the pieces, which were as the kisses of Huitzilopochtli, they shared in equal parts among the natives of Mexico and Tlatelolco . . . thus did they share among them the four parts of the body of Huitzilopochtli . . . in the districts each person ate a piece of the body of the god, and those who ate were young boys. . . ."[12]

It is surprising to notice how, just as with baptism and the remission of sins, investigators have usually given only passing attention to the fact that the Meso-american peoples practised the sacrament of communion. Yet it seems clear that the ceremony of sacrifice of *Unity* in *Multiplicity* can arise only from the principle of the redemption of matter, and must thus have its roots in a highly spiritual doctrine.

Here is an Aztec poem which confirms the existence of spiritual bonds between the individual and the Sun:

I offer, offer flowering cocoa:
that I may be sent to the House of the Sun!
Beautiful and very rich is the crown of quetzal plumes:
may I know the House of the Sun; may I go to that
  place!
Oh, no one contains in his soul the lovely inebriate
  flower:
sparse cocoa flowers giving their fragrance in
  Huexotzinco's water.
Each time the sun climbs this mountain
my heart cries and is sad:
would it were the flower of my heart; painted in
  beautiful colours!
The King of those who return sings of the flowers!

There is flowery intoxication; rejoice at the feast, oh ye
princes;
there is beautiful dancing: this is the House of Our
Father the Sun.

We stand on the turquoise wall:
the quetzal wood is surrounded;
he who dwells in Caves is by the water.
Here may it end at last, the plain of the serpent:
I carry over my shoulder a turquoise shield,
trembling in the wind the red flower of winter.[13]

The sun is called the *King of those who return*: it would be difficult to find more exact proof of the Nahuatl belief in the heavenly origin of the individual.

It can be seen, too, that the House of the Sun, which is no other than the firmament, is surrounded by turquoise and by quetzal plumes, precious things symbolizing the soul. So it speaks of a vision of the world of Unity in which the human soul at last enjoys the divine presence. It is clearly this same Unity which is represented in solar discs in which a circle of precious stones and another of feathers usually surrounds the symbol of the heavenly body.

The fact that the sky is described in the poem as the House of turquoise and of quetzal plumes corroborates our interpretation of the myth of Quetzalcoatl, because our hero laments that he has to leave exactly such houses:

"... Again the demons said to Quetzalcoatl, 'Son of mine, sing. Here is the song thou must sing.' And Ihuimecatl (one of the demons) sang: 'I shall depart from my house of quetzalli feathers, my house of jade."[14]

And when he had become aware of his new condition he sorrowfully expressed his nostalgia for lost unity:

"... It was an evil thing that one day I left my house. May those who are absent be sad. I took it for hardness and peril. May he who has a body of earth be and sing; I was not reared afflicted with servile labour."[15]

The absent ones whose sympathy he asks for can be none other than the inhabitants of the celestial world whence he has suddenly descended; his allusion to those who have a "body of earth" must be directed to those who have no recollection of their divine origin.

Nostalgia for lost Unity is the theme of most Nahuatl poetry. Here are some examples from Aztec documents:

The more I weep, the more I am afflicted,
the more my heart may not desire it,
have I not, when all is said, to go to the Land of the
Mystery?

Here on earth our hearts say:
"Oh my friends, would that we were immortal,
oh friends, where is the land in which one does not die?

Shall it be that I go? Does my mother live there? Does
my father live there?

In the Land of the Mystery . . . My heart shudders:
if only I had not to die, had not to perish . . .!
I suffer and feel pain.

Thou hast left thy fame already well-founded,
Oh Prince Tlacahuepantzin.
The fact is that here we are but slaves.
Men are simply standing
before him through whom everything lives.
Birth comes, life comes upon earth.
For a short while it is lent us,
the glory of that by which everything lives.
Birth comes, life comes upon earth.[16]

We come only to sleep,
We come only to dream:
It is not true, not true we come to live on the earth:

Spring grass are we become:

It comes, gloriously trailing, it puts out buds, our heart,
the flower of our bodies opens a few petals,
then withers![17]

Thy creation, thy protection dost thou extend, oh Giver of life.
There is no one can say misfortune will call him away from thy side!
Beautiful stones are giving birth
and quetzal feathers are opening:
perhaps they are thy heart, oh Giver of Life.
There is no one can say misfortune will call him away from thy side!
Maybe we live only there: Rejoice!
Only a short time can we be gathered together,
glory can be achieved always:
not one among men is thy friend.
For a little while thy flowers
are lent thee: dry flowers at last!
All that flowers in thy throne and thy company—
nobility, kingship, empire, in the midst of the plain—
is entwined with thy flowers: dry flowers at last![18]

As we have seen, the spiritual message of Quetzalcoatl deals with the resolution of the painful problem of human duality. The parable of the King of Tollan begins to speak of the principles of detachment and renunciation through which man can rediscover his own unity, and also lays the foundations of a priesthood. For the Aztecs, Quetzalcoatl was Lord of prayer and penitence:

> "... Quetzalcoatl did penance, piercing his legs and drawing blood with which he stained and made bloody the maguey spikes ... and this custom and order the priests and ministers of the Mexican idols took over as Quetzalcoatl had used it...."[19]

We know, besides, that in Tenochtitlan the high-ranking priests all took the title of Quetzalcoatl, and naturally this name, so constantly perpetuated through the centuries, was not the only factor uniting them with the founder of the Nahuatl religion. Until the close of the Empire the Meso-american prince-priests, thought to be reincarnations of Quetzalcoatl, performed rituals in which important moments from his mythical life were recalled. The German scholar, Eduard Seler, gives an example of such practices among the Zapotecs:

> "From Father Purgoa's description of how power was transmitted, it is evident that these priests were thought of as living images of the god of the Toltecs . . . Though chastity was imposed upon these priests . . . at certain feasts they were forced to become drunk and have relations with girls. If one of these became pregnant and gave birth to a son, this child was destined to succeed the chief priest. This is in accord with the story of Quetzalcoatl, priest-god of the Toltecs . . . who forgot his chastity in drunkenness . . . and for this sin was forced . . . not only to leave his city but also his country and to go toward the East where he raised a funeral pyre to destroy himself, and from the fire his heart rose to the heavens in the form of the planet Venus."[20]

After this sexual experience, the priests doubtless followed Quetzalcoatl's plan of liberation, and it is probable that once they had ceded their place to a successor they shut themselves in holy retirement ending in ritual death as symbolized by the redeeming fire.

The funeral ceremonies customary among the Aztecs seem also to have derived from Quetzalcoatl's doctrine. It was supposed that the dead man had to overcome seven difficult trials before reaching the desired end of his journey: the place where "the dead ended and were no more". At that moment, believing the dead no longer needed help, the survivors who had been performing the ritual put an end to their offerings. The seven trials—the last of which consisted in confronting the terrible god of the dead—lasted four years, and the place where "the dead ended and were no more" was reached only if they succeeded in escaping his rule. This much-desired moment is when the spirit, escaping the darkness of matter, finally rediscovers its origin in light; and death threatening to hold it back represents annihilation of the individual who comes with insufficient inner preparation. Various signs relate these trials to different stages in Quetzalcoatl's life after he had abandoned his capital. Among others there is the vast river on the road leading to liberation. Instead of crossing alone, Quetzalcoatl builds a bridge so that his "pages" or disciples can follow him. This bridge-building speaks once again of his mission to establish communication between earth and heaven, to unite man with god.

Whether fulfilled in life or after death, these rites re-enacting the parable of man changed into the planet must represent the trials attending man's passage to higher spiritual levels leading progressively closer to union with the transcendent. They must relate to secret rites of initiation in which the neophyte was prepared to receive the soul and learn to die, that is, to sacrifice his perishable self in order to be reborn into a regenerate life. Thus Nahuatl Mysteries, like those of all other traditions, had only one aim: that man be absorbed into god. For this reason the Meso-american peoples thought of Quetzalcoatl as man made god.

The practice of Initiation Mysteries explains an otherwise incomprehensible phenomenon in Nahuatl religion. At first sight it looks, according to Aztec texts, as if man's destiny in the other world were determined only by the accidental manner of his death. Sahagún tells how, besides the trials already mentioned, there existed:

> ". . . another place where they said the souls of the dead went, the earthly paradise named Tlalocan, in which it was said there was much rejoicing and comfort, and no sorrow whatever. . . . They go there who are killed by thunderbolts, drowned in water, those suffering from leprosy, sores, scabs, gout, hydropsy, those dying of contagious diseases; they do not burn, but bury the bodies of these sick people. . . . The other place, where the souls of the dead go, is the sky where

13 TEOTIHUATECAN DANCERS. Mexican National Museum

14 TEOTIHUATECAN DOLLS. Mexican National Museum

15 TEOTIHUATECAN MASK. Mexican National Museum

16 CHALCHIUHTLICUE, goddess of rivers. From Teotihuacan, now in the Mexican National Museum

> the sun lives. Those who go to heaven are those killed in wars and the prisoners who have died in their enemies' power. . . ."[21]

From these beliefs it has been deduced that the Nahuatls thought behaviour in life to have no consequence for the soul. This view completely contradicts what we know of the moral laws ruling in Tenochtitlan. According to such a view, for example, the over-riding need for penitence and purification dominating Aztec life would seem to have been only an incident, without roots in Nahuatl thought; yet actually it constituted its very essence.

In fact human existence was thought of as a preparation for death, which represented true birth achieved by becoming free from the finite, mortal self. It is probably in this sense that we must understand the curious expression ". . . the hour of parturition . . . is called the hour of death . . .",[22] because the newborn child must represent the tomb of the spirit which is opened only at the moment of the body's dissolution. On the other hand the Aztec wise men:

> ". . . said that they did not die but woke from a dream they had lived . . . and became once more spirits or gods. . . . They said, too, that some were transformed into the sun, others into the moon, and others into various planets . . ."[23]

It would seem that not all men achieved this glorious birth. Many of Sahagún's descriptions specify that only princes and high dignitaries were changed into spirits or stars, which indicates that the Initiation determining the soul's destiny was not accessible to all. Perhaps those who remained outside the Mysteries were those who went to the Earthly Paradise. As we have seen, the dead who went to this land of delight were merely buried, like the slaves sacrificed at the death of a great lord, whereas the latter were cremated and thus had access to the highest grades of Initiation.

It may be supposed that these Initiations were rigorously controlled by a religious order. The most important Order in ancient Mexico was that of the Knights Eagle and Tiger, which, though in Tenochtitlan it had assumed a predominantly warlike character, must originally have existed for the purpose of initiation into the sacred Mysteries. Later we shall give archaeological proofs of this, when we discuss the first Nahuatl centre where the eagle and tiger symbolism was clearly defined; but the data collected about this Order in the sixteenth century by the historian Muñoz Camargo also reveal its mystic origin:

> ". . . This ceremony of knighting the natives of Mexico and Tlaxcala and other provinces of the Mexican tongue, is worthy of note. . . . They knighted men with great ceremony, for first of all they were locked for forty or seventy days in a temple of their idols; and they fasted all that time and communicated with none but those who served them; at the end of that time they were taken to the Great Temple and were there given important doctrines of life which they must keep and guard; and before all this they taunted them, with many insulting and satirical words, and struck them, even in the face, with many reprimands. . . . Throughout their fast they did not wash. Before this they were all smeared and painted black, and with signs of deep humiliation that they should conceive and reach so great mercy and reward, watching over their arms throughout their fasting according to the ordinances, uses and customs so well kept among them. They were also in the habit of keeping the doors where they were fasting closed with branches of laurel, a tree much valued among the natives."[24]

As can be seen, the central part of these tests of Initiation is the detachment taught by Quetzalcoatl as a means of liberation from duality.

Taking advantage of this mystic aspiration to advance their own urge for power, the Aztecs replaced exaltation of spiritual life by physical death; and investigators have tended to think of their macabre artistic stylizations as an expression of Nahuatl thought. But archaelogical remains show that, far from having characterized all Meso-american peoples, such stylization is limited to the period of bloody conquests which began at the end of the tenth century with the arrival of the nomad hunters. In earlier centres, in place of such representations of death and of destructive gods, we find symbols of resurrection, a fact which should not surprise us, since Quetzalcoatl's transcendence is due precisely to his rôle as redeemer. This rôle, confirmed by all documents, is expressed in images of surprisingly suggestive power in the story of his visit to the Land of the Dead.

We have seen that after he had destroyed himself by fire, Quetzalcoatl remained eight days "underground". A fragment of this myth, from a manuscript dictated in Nahuatl shortly after the Conquest and published in Spanish under the title "Legend of the Suns", gives fuller details of this descent into Hell:

> "Then the gods took counsel and said, 'Who shall dwell here? The sky is fixed; and the Lady Earth, who shall dwell therein, oh gods?' They were all troubled.
>
> But there went Quetzalcoatl; he came to the Kingdom of the Dead, to the Lord and Lady of the Kingdom of the Dead. Thereupon he said: 'Behold why I have come. Thou art concealing precious bones. I have come to fetch them. But the King of the Dead told him: 'What wilt thou do, Quetzalcoatl?' And he answered again, 'The gods are troubled about who shall inhabit the earth.'
>
> The Lord of the Kingdom of the Dead said, 'It is well. Sound my snail trumpet, and four times bear it about the circle of my emerald throne.'
>
> But as the snail had no gimlet he called the worms. They made holes through which the wasps and night bees entered at once.
>
> Again said the Lord of the Kingdom of the Dead: 'It is well, take the bones!' But he told his vassals the dead: 'Yet tell him, oh gods, that he must leave them behind!' But Quetzalcoatl answered: 'No, I shall take them for ever.' But his double[25] said to him, 'Tell them I shall come to take them!' With this he was able to return upward, and he

took the precious bones. In one place were the bones of a man, in another of a woman. He gathered them up, he made a bundle, and he took them with him.

But again the Lord of the Dead said to his vassals: 'Gods, verily he has taken them, the precious bones. Come and dig him a hole.' They came and did so: he fell into the hole, churning the earth; the quail frightened him; he fell like one dead; and so he scattered the precious bones on the ground, and the quail pecked and ate them.

But Quetzalcoatl soon revived, wept over what had happened, and said to his double: 'My double, how shall this thing be?' And he said, 'How shall it be? It is true you have lost them. So be it!'

Then he gathered them up, picking them one by one, and made of them a bundle and took them to Tamoanohan.

And when he reached Tamoanohan, Quilaztli ground them down again; he threw the ground bones into a precious earthern pot, and upon them Quetzalcoatl threw his blood, taken from a living member, and then all the gods did penance, for which reason they said: 'Those worthy of the gods are born, since for us they did deserving penance.' "[26]

The blood with which Quetzalcoatl sprinkled the bones brought from the dead represents the divine fire which saves matter—we shall see later that blood and fire have the same symbolic significance—and it is clear that this myth speaks of the birth of man into spirituality.

But what is most remarkable about these narratives is the positive rôle they give to matter. It has been seen that if Venus must cross the earth to unite with the Sun, the King of Tollan sets out on his liberating voyage only after having committed the carnal act. Also, Quetzalcoatl does not succeed in his terrifying mission to the Land of the Dead until he as assumed the form of a dog and thanks to the worms and bees: that is, with the help of creatures who have no consciousness. This shows that, far from being a useless element that is only troublesome to the spirit, matter is necessary because it is only by the reciprocal action of one upon the other that liberation is achieved.

It would seem that if matter is saved by the spirit, the spirit in its turn has need of matter in order that it may be transformed into something like conscious energy, without which creation would cease to exist. Without this perpetual synthesis of contraries which man effects within himself, the world would disappear; for, just as with man, the danger menacing the Sun is simply that it may fall into the inertia of matter. It is a proof of this that during his nocturnal voyage—exactly at the moment when human aid is needed—the sun becomes a tiger and in that form is called Earth's Sun, in Nahuatl *Tlachitonatiuh*. This implies that the spirit falls fatally into matter, and can be saved only by the reconciliation of two opposed poles between which it swings. This hypothesis is also upheld by the Aztec Belief concerning the destiny of the souls of warriors. They used to say that after having met the rising sun, these formed a bodyguard across the sky but did not follow him to the west, that part of the world known as the "Land of Birth." These souls, being already the result of effort toward unification which is exactly the earthly test, were forever free from the dangers of duality.

The personality of Quetzalcoatl summarizes this vital synthesis. As Venus, he is pure spirit condemned to incarnation; as a dog (Xolotl) he is matter; and it is probably for the same reason that the Aztecs thought of him as the god of twins and other dual phenomena. In his third form he is the god who is the giver of breath which, setting in motion matter impregnated with spirit, allows the creation of luminous energy or soul.

This energy, indispensable to the movement of the universe, can only issue visibly from man, because only he is possessed of a centre susceptible of transforming his spirit. Without this dynamic point of union, spirit would be destined to lose itself in matter. By saving himself, man—of whom Quetzalcoatl is the archetype—saves Creation. This is why Quetzalcoatl is above all the Redeemer.

As the parable of the King of Tollan shows, this salvation is not easily achieved. To reconcile the matter and spirit of which he is formed, individual man must all his life keep up a painfully conscious struggle; he is a battle-ground in which two enemies confront each other pitilessly. The victory of one or other will decide whether he lives or dies; if matter conquers, his spirit is annihilated with him; if spirit wins, the body "flowers" and a new light goes to give power to the Sun. (The image of these flowers is the most frequent in Nahuatl literature; and it is expressly stated that the aim of the College in which the nobles were initiated into the mysteries of religion was to make "the body bloom and flower".)

In a later chapter we shall see that this "flowering" war, continually renewed in every conscious creature, is symbolized by two divergent currents, one of water, one of fire—which at last unite. We shall also see that the creation of all that exists on earth is the result of the active interpenetration of these two opposed elements.

The myth of the different Suns or Eras in the world only confirms these interpretations.

Four Suns were destroyed before the present one. The first, *Sun of Night*, or *Sun of Earth*, symbolized by a tiger, is clearly the reign of dark matter without hope of redemption. Alone among the four suns, none of its inhabitants can be saved: it is thus definitely sterile.

The second, represented by Quetzalcoatl as god of wind, is the *Sun of Air*, that is, of pure spirit destined to become incarnate. Its inhabitants are turned into monkeys.

Next comes the *Sun of Rain of Fire*, from which only the bird escape; and lastly the *Sun of Water*, from which the fishes arise.

Thus as long as these four life principles remain isolated they perish, because for creation—the only means of survival—a point of contact would be necessary in which one could act upon another dynamically.

That is why the Fifth Sun (five is the number of the centre) is the *Sun of Movement*, meeting in man. ". . . The name of this Sun is Naollin (Four Movements), now it is ours, by which today we live . . . It was the Sun of Quetzalcoatl. . . ."[27]

This sun, whose emblem is a human face, not only represents

the central region, but also what is above and what is below, that is, heaven and earth. The symbol of the world thus brought together is a cross.

It is interesting to observe that the fundamental creative principles in the Nahuatl religion are the same as those contained in the myth of the four burnt-out Suns. This proves that, in spite of having been taken as essential, they were not thought fit to live except by the creation of a centre in which their synthesis is established.

The parable of Venus teaches that this centre is in the heart of man, and that is why the supreme task of human existence is to wrest the heart from its condition of self-destructive multiplicity. Because of this belief the Aztecs were accustomed to place a precious stone in the mouths of the dead, to represent the heart emerging, brilliant and pure, from the fire consuming the body:

> ". . . They say that when the Lords and Nobles died they placed a green stone in their mouth . . . and they say this was the dead man's heart. . . ."[28]

It is due to this same belief that the most frequent sign symbolizing the Sun in Meso-american hieroglyphics is a precious stone.

This allows us the more easily to understand that the struggles, terrors and sacrifice of Quetzalcoatl during his perilous journey into Hell, and also the painful pilgrimage of the King of Tollan before he was made light, are images of the same revelation. In each case it is shown that only by plunging oneself into the very centre of matter—earth in the first case, body in the second—can one reach final reality. Only true knowledge allows movement toward inner profundity. Lord of knowledge, Quetzalcoatl sets off on his adventure that carries him to the world's edge—to the horizon where heaven and earth meet—through having become aware of the duality of his condition and the path he must take to free himself from it.

Given the essential analogy existing between nature and man, the latter, freeing his heart, becomes the craftsman perfecting the Universe, that is, Cosmic Unity. Meso-american cultures again and again describe the mystic formula expressing union between man and the *Whole*. The mathematical speculations known to have occupied a very important place in their studies were aimed at calculating the successive phases of union between the individual and the cosmic soul—between Venus and the Sun—phases that must gradually lead to complete Union.

The Aztec belief according to which the human Era will end and be replaced by the planets, probably indicates that the synthesis of opposites operating in man must one day reach completion, and that the kingdom of separation will then be forever superceded. It is perhaps because of this gigantic cosmic task that Quetzalcoatl's subjects called themselves the "Great Artificers" (Toltecas).

The ideas we have presented in this chapter are gathered together in the myth of the creation of the Fifth Sun, which, synthesizing all the rest, contains the whole spiritual basis of the Nahuatl religion. Here is the text of this fundamental myth in the form in which Sahagún found it:

> ". . . They used to say that before there was day in the world the gods met together . . . and said one to another: 'Who shall have the task of lighting the world?' Then to these words a god called Tecuzistecatl answered and said: 'I shall take charge of lighting the world.' Then again the gods spoke and said: 'Who else?' At that moment they looked at one another and conferred who should be the other, and none of them dared offer themselves for the task; they were all afraid and excused themselves. One of the gods to whom they were paying no attention, and who was afflicted with scabs, did not speak but listened to what the other gods said. The others spoke to him and said: 'Be thou he that shall light the world, scabby one,' and he with a good will obeyed what they ordered and answered: 'Mercifully I receive what ye order; so be it.' And then the two began to make penance for four days. Afterwards they lighted a fire in the hearth that was built in a rock. . . . Everything the god named Tecuzistecatl offered was precious, for instead of branches

he offered rich feathers . . . instead of pellets of hay he offered pellets of gold, instead of maguey thorns he offered thorns fashioned of precious stones: instead of bloody thorns he offered thorns of red coral, and the copal he offered was good. The scabby one, who was called Nanautzin, instead of branches offered green canes tied three by three, amounting to nine in all; he offered pellets of hay and maguey thorns and he anointed them with his own blood, and instead of copal he offered the scabs of his sores . . . to each of these gods they built a tower like a mountain; in these mountains they did penance for four nights . . . then they threw them the jars and all the other things with which they had done penance. This was done at the end . . . of their penance when the next night, at midnight, they had to begin their tasks; when the fire had burned for four days . . . the gods arranged themselves in two ranks, some on one side of the fire, some on the other, and then the two above-mentioned placed themselves before the fire, facing it, in the midst of the two ranks of gods, all standing, and then they spoke and said to Tecuzistecatl: 'Ea, Tecuzistecatl, enter thou into the fire!' And then he prepared to throw himself into it; and as the fire was large and burning greatly, he felt great heat, was afraid, and dared not throw himself in, but turned away. Again he turned to throw himself into the flames, gathering strength, but reaching it he stopped; four times he tried, but never dared throw himself in. There was a law that none should try more than four times. So when he had tried four times the gods then spoke to Nanautzin, and said to him: 'Ea, then, Nanautzin, try thou.' And when the gods had spoken to him he made an effort and closed his eyes, and rushed forward, and cast himself into the fire, and then he began to crackle and burn in the fire like one roasting. When Tecuzistecatl saw he had cast himself into the fire and was burning, he rushed forward and threw himself into the flames. . . ."[29]

It is scarcely necessary to emphasize that in this myth are the beginnings of the whole doctrine of Quetzalcoatl. As in the parable of the King of Tollan, light comes from the sacrificial fire; and the same emphasis is laid on purification, humility and renunciation. We see that the chosen one of the gods is the scabby one, he whose body is disintegrating, that is, the one who having completed his task of reconciling the opposites has begun to be detached from his fragmentary self.

This tale, with its ritual details and secret formulae, seems to constitute the model for the final trial of Initiation, which leads through death to eternal life.

But what is so astonishing is the cosmic rôle assigned to moral virtue: the Sun which gives life to the universe is born of man's sacrifice and can subsist only if sustained by inner power. In fact in this myth it is the individual who brings about universal salvation, and this indicates that the movement initiating the Fifth Sun is spirituality. So by a different road we once again arrive at the conclusion that the Era of Quetzalcoatl is that of the advent of the soul, the unifying centre which, according to our understanding, is the very essence of all religious thought.

The meaning of the second part of the myth leads us to the same conclusion:

> ". . . When the sun began to rise it seemed very red and it lurched from side to side and none could look at it, for it took sight from the eyes, it shone, and threw out rays splendidly, and its rays spilt everywhere; and afterwards the moon rose in the same part of the east, on a par with the sun; first the sun, and behind it the moon. And those who tell tales say that they had the same light shining, and the gods saw that they shone equally, and they spoke again and said: 'Oh gods, how can this be? Is it well that they go side by side? Is it well they shine equally?' And the gods pronounced sentence and said: 'Be it so.' And then one of them went running, and flung a rabbit in Tecuzistecatl's face, and his face darkened, his splendour was put out, and his face remained as it is now. After both had risen upon earth, they were still, not moving from one place, the sun and moon; and again the gods spoke and said: 'How can we live? Does the sun not wag? Must we live among the lowly? Let us all surround him that he revive through our death.' And then

the air set to killing all the gods, and killed them, and it is said that one named Xolotl refused death and said to the gods: 'Oh Gods, I shall not die!' And he cried in such a manner that his eyes became swollen with tears, and when he came to the one who was killing he began to run away; he hid in the maize stalks and turned himself into a maize root with two stalks . . . and he was seen and discovered, and again he began to run away and he hid among the maguey and turned himself into a maguey with two bodies; again he was seen, and he began to run away and threw himself into the water and turned into a fish named *axolotl*, and from there they took and killed him; and they say that though the gods were dead the sun did not therefore move; and then the wind began to blow with a strong blast, and made the sun move on its course. . . ."[30]

This motionless sun so splendidly shining, that made them lose their sight, seems to have been the mass of cosmic spirit in its pure state, before any communion, any plunging into matter, had taken place. Only the sacrifice of the gods—that is, of men capable of sacrifice—and the breath of Quetzalcoatl—manage to stir the sun; this makes one think that without such intervention the Fifth Sun would have been no more capable of life than the previous ones that had been annihilated.

As we have shown earlier, the danger menacing the Sun is inertia. Only the movement taking place in man's heart between two contraries that must be harmonized will save Creation from this mortal danger.

As to the episode about Xolotl—twin brother of Quetzalcoatl and deity of dual phenomena—who refuses to die; this may perhaps be a hint of the multifarious relations that can be established between matter and spirit.

We have now briefly examined all the texts relevant to our discussion. Undoubtedly these texts still hide innumerable secrets: much patience and love will be necessary if they are ever to be unearthed.

In the hope of establishing some points of reference upon

which future investigations can be based, let us now try to verify the correctness of the interpretations we have put forward in this section. To do so, we shall have to analyse carefully the glyphs of the symbolic language of the Nahuatl religion as they are found on all known sites of this civilization, from the earliest to the latest. Only if the meaning of the symbols tallies with those of the mythical accounts can our hypotheses be taken as proved.

NOTES

1. Elsie Clew Parsons, *Mitla, Town of Souls,* pp. 324 and 329.
2. Laurette Séjourné, *Una Interpretacion de las Figurillas del Arcaico,* Revista Mexicana de Estudios Antropológicos, Vol. XIII, i, Mexico, 1952.
3. Sahagún, op. cit., Vol. I, p. 571.
4. *Ibid.,* p. 602.
5. The Nahuatl word for the place where the heavenly pair abide, *Tlacapillachiualoya,* means "place where the children of men are made".
6. Sahagún, op. cit., Vol. I, p. 608.
7. *Anales de Cuauhtitlán,* Codice Chimalpopoca, Imprenta Universitaria, Mexico, 1945, p. 7.
8. *Ibid.,* p. 9.
9. "The west is mankind's first country, its birthplace." Seler.
10. Sahagún, op. cit., Vol. I, p. 457.
11. *Ibid.*
12. *Ibid.,* pp. 290-2.
13. Angel María Garibay, "Romances de la Muerte", *Las Letras Patrias,* No. 2, Mexico, 1954, p. 18.
14. *Anales de Cuauhtitlan,* op. cit., pp. 9, 10, 11.
15. *Ibid.*
16. Angel María Garibay, *Las Letras Patrias,* No. 2, Mexico, 1954, p. 12.
17. Angel María Garibay, *Historia de la Literatura Nahuatl,* Editorial Porrua, S.A., Mexico, 1953, p. 91.
18. *Ibid.,* p. 148.
19. Sahagún, op. cit., Vol. I, p. 296.

20. Eduard Seler, Bulletin 28, Smithsonian Institution, Washington, 1904, p. 276.
21. Sahagún, op. cit., Vol. I, p. 318.
22. *Ibid.*, Vol. I, p. 599.
23. *Ibid.*, Vol. II, p. 309.
24. Diego Muñoz Camargo, *Historia de Tlaxcala*, Mexico, 1948, pp. 56-8.
25. Quetzalcoatl's double is the dog Xolotl.
26. *Leyendas de Los Soles*, translated from the Nahuatl by Angel María Garibay and inserted into his *Historia de la Literatura Nahuatl*, Editorial Porrua, Mexico, 1953, pp. 295-6.
27. *Leyenda de Los Soles*, op. cit., p. 121.
28. Sahagún, op. cit., Vol. I, p. 317.
29. *Ibid.*, Vol. II, pp. 12-14.
30. *Ibid.*, Vol. II, pp. 15, 16.

PART III

Nahuatl Symbolic Language

I

ANCIENT TOLLAN

AT THE END of the archaic period known as "formative" because it immediately precedes the flowering of the higher Meso-american cultures, appears the fire god, oldest of the Nahuatl deities. He makes his appearance in the same form in which he was revered much later by the Aztecs: as an old man with wrinkled face and carrying a brazier on his head.

Images of this ancient deity have been discovered in the earliest known Meso-american temple—Cuicuilco, a circular edifice situated on the outskirts of present-day Mexico City and found buried beneath eight metres of lava.

For a long time these first manifestations of a religious spirit seem to have remained unique, because the temple itself, and also the god Huehueteotl (*Huehue*, old; and *Teotl*, god), are the only expressions of the divine cult that have been found in Cuicuilco. The archaeological remains discovered at this site consist of magical representations of humans and of animals. They are devoid of symbolism and differ in no way from the remains of earlier periods. The only exceptions to this are the two or three images of this ancient god that have been unearthed.

It is not known how long this ritual centre existed, but it was eventually destroyed by the eruption of a volcano. With the help of comparative studies it has been possible to establish that this centre ceased to exist as far back as the last few centuries before the beginning of our era.[1] Since all its cultural characteristics—the ceramics, the archaic figurines, the Fire God, and the manner of construction—are otherwise found only in

Teotihuacan (fifty kilometres from Mexico City), it may be deduced that this Teotihuacan came into existence soon afterwards and sprang directly from the earlier centre.

So Teotihuacan rests upon archaic foundations. Very soon, however, the tender seed transplanted from Cuicuilco took root in the new soil and blossomed luxuriantly into the Nahuatl religion in all its richness. While artists were painting and carving the religious symbolic language in this huge sacred metropolis, the whole body of knowledge which characterizes Meso-american civilization developed into its final form.

The origins of this high culture are a complete mystery. Because of the appearance of certain tropical motifs, such as serpents, quetzal birds, tropical sea-shells and turtles, it has been thought to have come from the south; but though they may originally have emanated from other zones, these motifs are so strongly integrated into the spiritual unity of Teotihuacan that it is impossible to suppose they could have been transplanted there already converted into symbols. Of course the species represented must have been familiar to the Teotihuatecans, but archaeology has shown that the peoples of these regions used to travel extensively. We cannot, however, just for this reason presuppose that elaborate cultural forms were transferred from one region to another, especially since the characteristic Nahuatl symbolism is not known to have existed anywhere else at this period. Yet it existed in Teotihuacan in exactly the same form in which the Aztecs revived it centuries later.

Teotihuacan, the oldest metropolis in Meso-america, is also the only one possessing a continuous history from the archaic through to the purely classical period. At other sites excavation has revealed two phases, each consisting of a number of different layers and so completely distinct one from the other that they have been attributed to unrelated peoples. It is only in the second phase that traces of specific, differentiated cultures have been found; from this it follows that by the time the Mayan[2] or Zapotec[3] cities were beginning to develop their special characteristics in the south, Teotihuacan was already rising firm upon its foundations and had developed the religion, arts and sciences that were to prevail for more than fifteen centuries. Although they fail to explain Teotihuacan's ascendancy over the whole of ancient Mexico—an ascendancy that springs rather from its incomparable genius—these simple chronological data nevertheless help us to find our way through the labyrinth of Mesoamerican societies.

We shall do well to remember that in Nahuatl the word Tollan means "great city or metropolis", and that all the capitals of the high plateau bore this name besides one peculiar to themselves. Being the archetype of all that were to come, Teotihuacan is usually called simply Tollan, as it is in certain ancient maps. In a study of the most important of these, Aubin, the French student of ancient America, says that the site of Teotihuacan:

> ". . . bears the name Tollan . . . and not Teotihuacan . . . this apparent anomaly, repeated to a certain extent in the Xolotl Codex, may arise from the fact that, according to one translator of a history of Teotihuacan which I shall publish, this city would have been given a Toltec name by the Toltec founders whose metropolis it was, 'as Rome', says the translator, 'is that of the Christians.' "[4]

Learned Aztecs who transmitted their knowledge either in writing or by informing the Spanish Chroniclers directly, agree with the archaeological findings about this Tollan, which they considered to be the source of their knowledge and their history. Thus in order to calculate the antiquity of the Nahuatls, Sahagún, from the very first pages of his book, fixes the date of this primordial city:

> "As to the antiquity of this people, it is proven that for more than two thousand years they have lived in this land now called New Spain, because through their ancient pictures there is evidence that the famous city called Tollan was destroyed a thousand years ago or very nearly . . . and as to the time it took to build it and the time it prospered before it was destroyed, it is consonant with truth that over a

17 XOCHIPILLI, Lord of Flowers. Aztec sculpture. Mexican National Museum

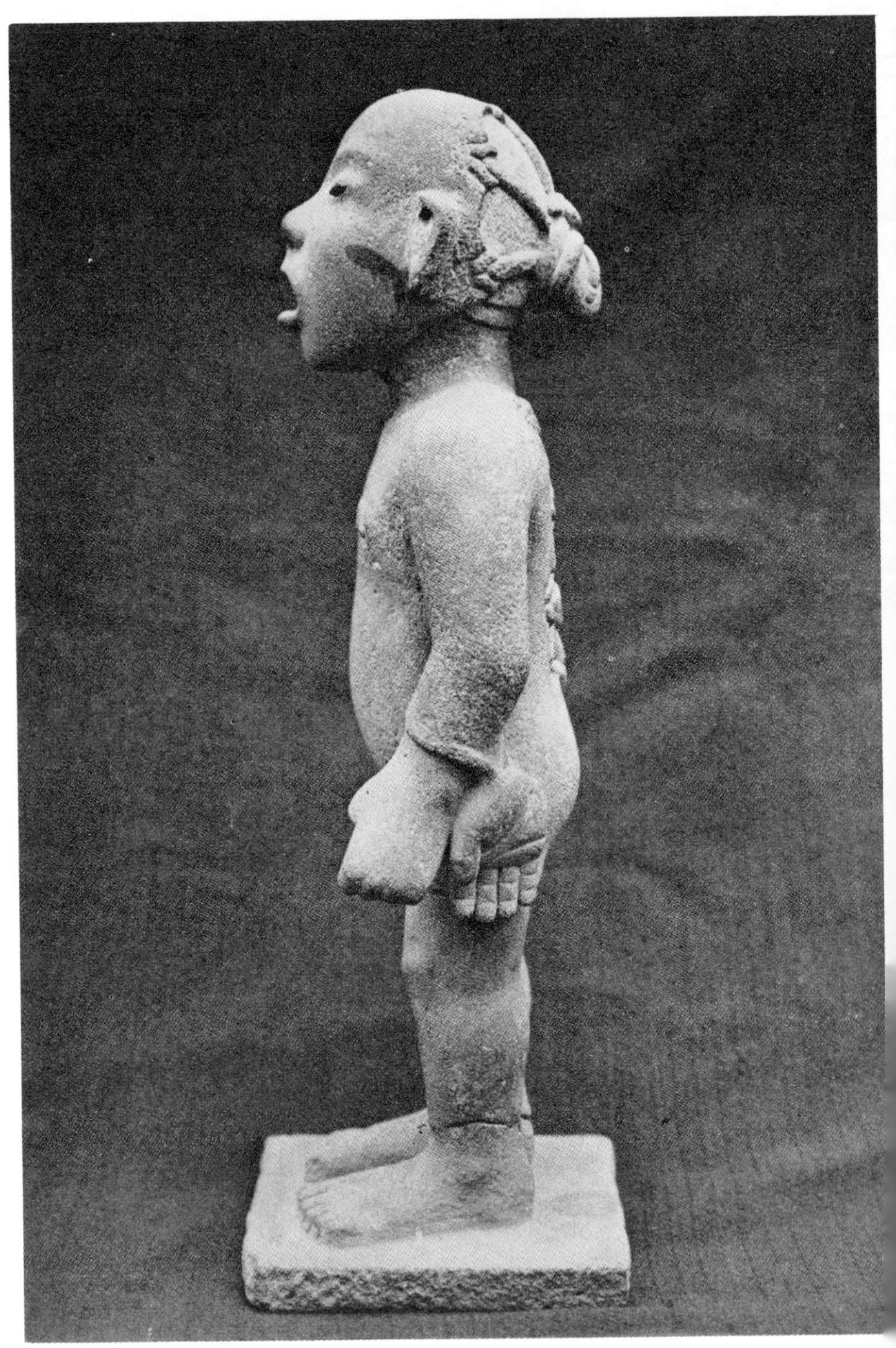

18 XIPE, the Flayed God. Aztec sculpture. In a private collection

thousand years passed, from which it follows that this land was populated at least five hundred years before the Incarnation of our Redeemer. This famous and great city of Tollan, very rich and well-ordered, very wise and powerful, suffered the adverse fortune of Troy."[5]

The chronology established by excavation merely confirms these calculations.

The facts, moreover, agree with what the chroniclers always affirm: that the king of Tollan was Quetzalcoatl, creator of all human wisdom. Archaeology establishes that Teotihuacan is not only the place where the Nahuatl culture was created, but also the first—for long the only—centre where the cult of Quetzalcoatl found expression (Quetzal: bird; coatl: serpent). By the fourth century Teotihuacan already possessed great buildings profusely ornamented with plumed serpents, an image till that time entirely unknown.

The archaeological proof that the plumed serpent did not exist before Teotihuacan, and that similar images found in other zones are later in date, is not a mere technical detail: it is the scientific argument proving that Teotihuacan was the first Nahuatl city.

We insist on this point because in 1941 American historians held a congress in which, after various stormy sessions, they passed a resolution stating that the capital of Quetzalcoatl was not Teotihuacan, as investigators of the eminence of Eduard Seler had believed, but a certain Tollan Xicotitlan (Tula, 125 miles from Mexico City), which dates back only to the tenth century, that is, to a moment when Meso-america suffered the brutal shock of mass invasion from nomad hunters and had strayed far from the mysticism of earlier epochs.

We shall not here enter into detailed speculations on this point. Elsewhere we have affirmed our certainty that, in the light of archaeological material available today, such a resolution cannot be maintained.[6] Not only have the technical details upon which it rested become obsolete, but ten seasons of explorations in Tula-Xicotitlan[7] have unearthed a second-rate civic centre which, except for a few remarkable sculptures, contains only crude copies of imported motifs and thus cannot possibly have been the cradle of a glorious culture.[8]

It is disconcerting to find that most of the students who prefer to think of Tula-Xicotitlan as Quetzalcoatl's home have ignored the fact that images of the god already existed in a city nearly a thousand years older. It is as if we were to place the life of Christ and the beginning of our Christian Era in the tenth century and were to ignore the existence of earlier historical material and representations of the crucifix before that date. In order to overcome the obstacle, some students have tried to maintain that the formalized plumed serpent of Teotihuacan is merely one among other signs representing water. But this thesis, which would be equivalent to placing the Christian symbolism of the crucifix before Christianity, is unacceptable. Everything points to the plumed serpent being a symbol whose meaning penetrates far deeper than the representation of some object in nature.

Quetzalcoatl taught that human greatness grows out of the awareness of a spiritual order; his image must therefore be the symbol of this truth. The serpent plumes must be speaking to us of the spirit which makes it possible for man—even while his body, like the reptile's, is dragged in the dust—to know the superhuman joy of creation. They are thus, as it were, a song to the most exalted inner freedom. This hypothesis is confirmed by the Nahuatl symbolism where the serpent represents matter—being always associated with terrestrial gods—and the bird heaven. The plumed serpent is thus the sign of the revelation of the heavenly origin of man.

II

TEOTIHUACAN: CITY OF THE GODS

It seems, because of its sudden emergence and creative vigour, that Teotihuacan must have been fashioned in the full glare of this revelation. It is like a vast poem, every detail an integral part of a highly inspired whole.

Surprisingly, no earlier examples of its principal motifs have been discovered, and its standards remained essentially unchanged until the time of the Spanish conquest. But if it is hard to believe that some of its cultural characteristics—such as its architectural style, the orientation of its buildings, and details of sculptures and paintings—can have assumed their final shape right from the start, it is still more difficult to imagine how the system of thought upon which it is based could have appeared suddenly in a state of perfect development. There is no single trace to show how this prodigious work was elaborated. Was it a collective task, or that of one single man? The unchallenged position held by Quetzalcoatl seems to suggest the second hypothesis. However this may be, and in spite of the fact that Teotihuacan has its roots deep in the archaic world, it is clear that only a vision of the vastness of the human spirit—of the divine spark uniting and harmonizing—could possibly have given birth to the dynamic power that must have presided over the founding of a city such as this, built to the glory of the plumed serpent—that is, to conscious man.

It is significant that the name of this first metropolis is "City of the Gods" (the meaning of the Nahuatl word, Teotihuacan). Sahagún tells us it was so called because:

> ". . . The Lords therein buried, after their deaths were canonized as gods, and it was said that they did not die, but wakened out of a dream they had lived; this is the reason why the ancients say that when men died they did not perish but began to live again, waking almost out of a dream, and that they turned into spirits or gods . . . and so they said to the dead: 'Lord or Lady, wake, for it begins to dawn, now comes the daylight for the yellow-feathered birds begin to sing, and the many-coloured butterflies go flying'; and when anyone died, they used to say of him that he was now *teotl*, meaning to say he had died in order to become spirit or god."[9]

Thus, far from implying any gross, polytheistic belief, the term Teotihuacan evokes the idea of human divinity and shows that the City of the Gods was the very place where the serpent learned miraculously to fly; that is, where the individual, through inner growth, attained to the category of a celestial being.

The metropolis is constructed for this purpose. Its ritual centre is divided into two sections, heaven and earth, joined at its axis by a vast ascending avenue. At its highest extremity, thirty metres above the lower, are the pyramids of the sun and moon, and innumerable other buildings so far unexcavated. At the lower end an area four hundred metres square constitutes the temple of Quetzalcoatl.[10] The heavenly section is composed of masses rising skyward; the earthly is a harmonious series of horizontal lines. The pyramid of the Sun (Plate 1) seems to pierce the sky, whereas the home of the plumed serpent (Plate 2) appears to be at rest on the earth.

In accord with Nahuatl cosmology, all the monuments are orientated in relation to the sun. This orientation has an interesting detail. The east-west axis which, since it represents the trajectory of the drama of the incarnation and liberation, was used as the point of orientation throughout Meso-america, lies seventeen degrees north of the true line. After detailed investigations the architect Ignacio Marquina discovered that the cause of the displacement arises because the pyramid points toward the spot where the sun falls below the horizon on the day of its passage through the sky's zenith.

There are doubtless various esoteric explanations for this preference, but the most obvious is that, since the zenith is the centre of the firmament, the sun when it reaches this point becomes the heart of the universe, and this is an attribute belonging to Quetzalcoatl's sun. That is to say, the pyramid is dedicated to the Fifth Sun, which was expressly created in Teotihuacan. The seventeen-degree shift to the north has thus so fundamental a meaning that this orientation was used until Aztec times.

The quadrangle of Quetzalcoatl is surrounded by platforms six metres high, supported by the pedestals of sanctuaries that split up the whole surface into rhythmic parts (Plate 3).

The rear section of the quadrangle is a pyramid-shaped building completely covered with plumed serpents. The ramps of the stairway leading to the sanctuary which once crowned it are studded with great serpent heads.[11] The plane surfaces above the sloping walls have, superimposed over relief carvings of the symbolic reptile, a series of heads of Quetzalcoatl and of Tlaloc, the rain god, alternating one with another (Plates 4 and 5). These two heads are different symbolic expressions of one and the same basic concept of the Nahuatl religion: the vital impulse arising from the unification of opposing elements. Later we shall see that, like Quetzalcoatl, Tlaloc is the bearer of the luminous seed which converts matter—in this case the earth—into creative energy.

All this suggests that the place may well have been the Calmecac, "the house where the body buds and flowers," as the Aztecs called the religious college where the nobility was educated. This supposition is reinforced by the fact that the Calmecac in Tenochtitlan was under Quetzalcoatl's patronage and that the teaching there professed derived entirely from his doctrine. The numerous and till now unexplored dwellings surrounding the pyramid must have been places of retreat for the disciples and for their spiritual guides.

The ascent of the holy avenue must doubtless have been performed at the last stage of initiation, and we may imagine it to have been accompanied by a profound solemnity.

The road that had to be traversed, two kilometres long and forty metres wide, was marked out by terraces flanked by buildings where the neophyte may have had to pause and go through ceremonies representing the pilgrimage of Quetzalcoatl toward the orient. It is significant that the temple of the Sun is situated at the eastern end of this avenue, which was called "street of the dead" (Miccaotli), a name probably deriving from the fact that the initiate first suffered a ritual death before proceeding along it to the Sun.[12]

If we remember that Quetzalcoatl left his kingdom only after an experience that has all the appearance of a death through initiation—four days enclosed in a stone coffin—we may suppose that the neophyte took the road of Miccaotli only after symbolically abandoning his earthly swaddling clothes.

The neophyte had finally to climb the pyramid of the Sun, seventy-five metres high and formed of extremely narrow superimposed steps. It was probably at the summit of this artificial mountain that by means of redeeming fire the initiate penetrated into the luminous consciousness of the heavenly bodies.

Today the City of the Gods betrays nothing of the mystic ardour that must have fired the men who once lived there. Further south, in the land of the Maya, the monuments were closely integrated with the life of the forest and have preserved their character in a remarkable way. But the original physiognomy of Teotihuacan has been utterly lost because of the nature of the surrounding country. Before the Spaniards arrived it had already been covered with earth, and it still lies for the most part beneath labour camps.

Because of the grey mantle which covers it, and the fact that most of its sculptured stones have been taken for the construction of churches in the surrounding valley, and that the paintings which once adorned its ritual centre have disappeared, an impenetrable air of severity has today replaced its ancient splendour.

Reduced to a schematic purity, these sombre, colourless buildings, like ascetic bodies devoid of all passion, speak today with inhuman harshness of the spiritual formulae which created them. They have been despoiled of the symbolic poetry which, with the help of form and colour, once revealed their hidden truths. They are now so naked as to appear merely the result of mathematical calculations elaborated from some rigid numerical law imposed upon man by the stars.

The archaeological area of Teotihuacan has unfortunately been so little explored that the data indispensable for a study of this law are not available, and only a few aspects of it are comprehensible to us.[13]

As we have seen, the city is constructed entirely according to the orientation of the pyramid of the Sun. This clearly shows how important to its founders was the annual cycle. Its importance is still further emphasized by the fact that 365 heads in high relief adorned Quetzalcoatl's temple, and by the existence among the symbols of a sign representing a year. Moreover, the cult of Venus demanded that a calendar of its revolutions be calculated and used.

The arrangement of space and buildings also suggests that the same numerical law strictly determined the plans. For example, if we examine different parts of the ceremonial centre, we see that these are always composed of rectangles and triangles: large square courtyards enclosing a pyramid, a shape which in its turn is simply a rectangle crowned with a triangle. As essentially the same shapes are used for the symbol of a year (Plate 7), this geometry may well be significant if we can only discover its meaning. We shall try to interpret it with the help of the symbolic Nahuatl language, the only instrument we have for studying these distant things.

III

THE LAW OF THE CENTRE

Although it appears with many variations, the most familiar Nahuatl symbol is composed basically of four points—the sign for solar heat—placed about a centre. We have seen that the number 5 represents the centre, and that it is also the point where heaven and earth meet; this fact has been fully demonstrated by Eduard Seler. To be more exact we should say that this five-fold figure, or quincunx, is also the precious jewel symbolizing the heart, the meeting-place of opposed principles. Thus we see united in a single sign all the characteristics of the Fifth Sun, or heavenly heart, which are also manifest in the mythology.

It is obvious that the quincunx is simply the stylized representation of the square surmounted by the triangle, its centre being the apex of the pyramid reduced to a plane. (If from each

Fig. 1. This face, symbolizing the Fifth Sun, alternates with the sign of Venus (right) to frame a door in one of the palaces of Teotihuacan.

of the four corners of a square we draw a line to a centre above, we obtain a pyramid.) It is clear, therefore, that not only the myths but also the symbolism of Teotihuacan expresses the idea of the four primordial elements redeemed by a unifying centre, a concept which is the kernel of Nahuatl thought and which determines all its most important manifestations. As Alfonso Caso emphasizes: "... This fundamental idea of the four cardinal points and the central area (below and above) which forms the fifth or central area, is found in all the religious expressions of the Aztec people..."[14]

The quincunx is a model of concise expression, and contains even more meanings than the above. It has been fully demonstrated that the synodic revolutions of Venus, 584 days, played a fundamental rôle in Meso-america. The chief use of the calculations in Mayan glyphs and codices, for example, is to register both the past and future conjunctions of this planet with the sun over considerable periods of time. Since Venus-years are computed in groups of five (corresponding to eight solar years), the number 5 is also the symbol for Venus, that is, for Quetzalcoatl.

The whole system is very remarkably constructed. Is not the Fifth Sun that of the man-god whose heart was transformed into the planet Venus? And is it not precisely Quetzalcoatl who

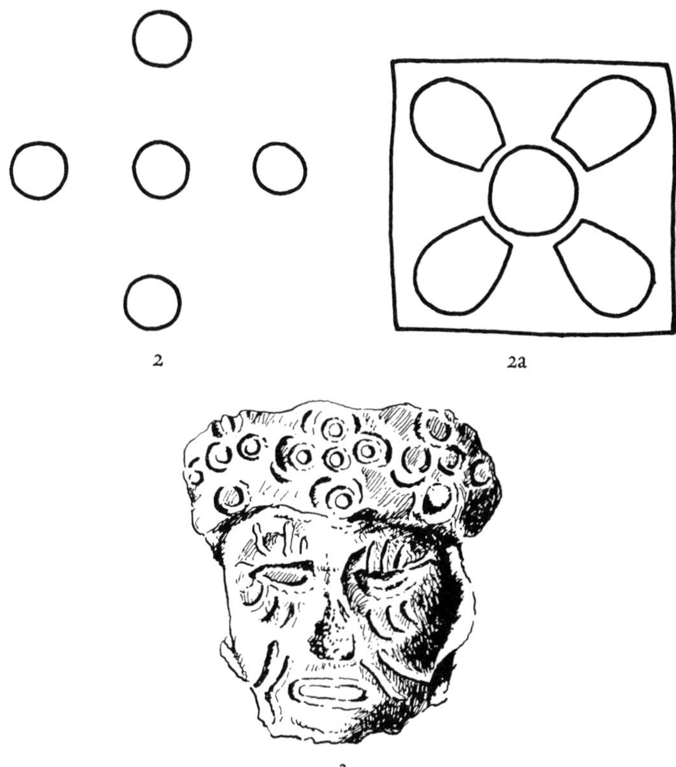

Fig. 2. The five points in a cross or quincunx. 2a. The five points enclosed in a square. The quincunx is the most frequently occurring sign in the Meso-american symbolic language. In the form 2a it occurs more than fifty times on one of the most famous of Aztec solar monuments (see fig. 4).

Fig. 3. The quincunx can here be clearly seen on the headdress of the Teotihuatecan Fire God.

inaugurated the Era of the Centre, thus disclosing the existence of a force capable of freeing the world from inertia?

But the quincunx also accompanies the god of fire, who is god of the centre and is therefore called "the earth's umbilicus". Under the name of Xiuhtecutli he represents the Lord of the Year, or the Lord of the Precious Jewel. All this confirms that the principle of the Law of the Centre, symbolized by the Fifth Sun, is thought of as the element light-heat, dynamically united with matter.

In spite of sadly insufficient exploration, archaeological research does enable us to see that Teotihuacan reflects the image of infinite cycles, within which the Law of the Centre prevents the splitting asunder of opposing forces. These cycles, based upon the revolutions of the planets and upon laborious calculations, include the simplest—the yearly death and resurrection of Nature—and spread outward to embrace immense units. These great time cycles correspond to the mystic search for moments of supreme liberation, that is, of union between the individual and the cosmic soul, time and eternity, the finite and the infinite.

It is probable that not a single detail in the City of the Gods was left to chance, and that the astronomical computations which the Mayans loved to inscribe on their monuments and in their books are implicit in every measurement, every line, and every ornament (Fig. 1). The exact precision with which Nahuatl thought is expressed in mythology and symbolism would have been impossible without the previous existence of an exact science. To understand this, we have only to imagine the speculative process needed to comprise a whole metaphysical treatise within a single image. In order to form some idea of this process, let us try and trace a few of the variants of the quincunx.

Its most simple expression consists of five points, either enclosed or not in a square (Figs. 2 and 2a). These symbolize the precious jewel, emblem of the Sun, the human heart, and heat. Fig. 2 is a detail from an image of the god of fire in Teotihuacan (Fig. 3); Figure 2a occurs more than fifty times on one of the most famous Aztec solar monuments (Fig. 4).

If the four outer points, instead of being represented by circles, are cut away, then the space between them takes shape and appears in the form of a cross (Fig. 5). This is the commonest form of the quincunx. It occurs on the image of a fire god (Fig. 6); on an Aztec representation of Quetzalcoatl (Fig. 7); and on a Sun Eagle (Fig. 8). Without the surrounding line, this cross

Fig. 4. Aztec image of a cosmic cycle. In the centre, the Fifth Sun represented as in Teotihuacan, surrounded by symbols of the previous eras. Two fire serpents form the outer circle; their fiery character is suggested by the starred volutes seen on the human heads in the lower part of the figure, and by the butterfly motif on their bodies. (Mexican National Museum.)

(Fig. 9) is characteristic of fire—it is invariably found on Aztec braziers and incense burners—and of Quetzalcoatl.

The same stylized cross, with the points of the quincunx clearly marked, is the characteristic sign for Venus, the Morning Star (Fig. 10).

When it means *Movement*, the Fifth Sun is represented by

two divergent lines forming four poles in opposition and uniting at the centre (Fig. 11).

But the all-powerful Law of the Centre is expressed not only by the concise quincunx. It is the axis of Quetzalcoatl's religion, and really regulates the whole of Nahuatl symbolism, the latter illustrating or elucidating the different stages in the continuous process of transfiguration to which the creative union, between matter and spirit is subjected at its centre.

Because the supreme Reality lives at the very centre of matter, the variety of forms assumed by Nature in her animal and vegetable kingdoms are considered, so to speak, as the clothing or outer manifestations of this Reality. They differ among themselves only in the levels of consciousness which they are capable of reaching.

Just as on earth the divine spark engenders life in all its rich variety, so the quincunx, seed of a revealed cosmology, blossoms in a dazzling series of images. Since they belong to the universe of forms, these images often appear deceptively simple. We hope to be able to show that the truth is quite otherwise.

IV

THE PAINTINGS OF TEOTIHUACAN

What is today the most forbidding of all archaeological cities was in its lifetime so magnificent that it was held in loving memory to the end of pre-Spanish times. The radical change that took place in its outer appearance is due especially to the fact that painting was its principal mode of expression. Owing to the fragility of these murals once they had become exposed to the elements, the Great Tollan, formerly unequalled in its dazzling shapes and colours, faded away, and slowly through the centuries became reduced to its bare outlines.

But although the paintings on the pyramids are by now only pale, washed-out lines, there still remain traces in which their

Fig. 5. In Nahuatl hieroglyphics this form of quincunx is called 'The Cross of Quetzalcoatl'; in Mayan it is the 'Cross of Kan' (*Kan*, yellow).

Fig. 6. The Cross of Quetzalcoatl on the headdress of a Fire God. From the *Cerro de las Mesas,* Veracruz. (Mexican National Museum.)

Fig. 7. The Cross on Quetzalcoatl's shield. (Codex Florentine).

Fig. 8. Eagle bearing the Cross of Quetzalcoatl, which is the bird's eye. Obsidian object excavated in La Venta, Tabasco. (Mexican National Museum.)

original brilliance can be admired. They are to be found in the palaces around the ritual centre, this being the heart of the city, and are spread over an area of several kilometres.[15] Their preservation is due to the custom, probably a religious one, of burying one building and erecting another above it. The walls of the earlier building used to be demolished to a height of about one metre, and the rubble would then be used to fill surfaces no longer required. In this way the later building would seal off the earlier one. As the walls were invariably covered with frescoes, these are preserved in the form of innumerable fragments and some intact paintings. Still vibrating with their ancient life, they revive today the mysteries of the Nahuatl religion.

Judging by the number of stucco floors that are found everywhere, and by the quantities of ceramics, figurines and jewelled objects which the inhabitants of this area sell surreptitiously today, there must be a vast number of these residences still buried underground. One frequently hears of somebody with scraps of paintings to sell, and it was this commercial habit which in 1942 set archaeologists on the trail of treasures far more important to Pre-columbian history than anything discovered for years past.

Fig. 9 (left). The Cross of Quetzalcoatl as it appears in pictures of the New Fire Ceremony in the Codex Borbonicus.

Fig. 10 (right). The symbol for Venus in Teotihuatecan and Mayan hieroglyphic writing.

Fig. 11. Different versions of the hieroglyph *movement* (*a, b, c,* Teotihuatecan; *d,* Codex Borgia; *e,* Codex Florentine; *f,* Codices Borbonicus and Borgia.)

Up to now only three of these palaces have been even partially explored. Although the material obtained represents an infinitesimal part of what each single palace might yield, sensational documents have already been brought to light. Even before they had been deciphered, these frescoes confirmed historic references to ancient Tollan. In "A Toltec Elegy", for example, the paintings are listed among its vanished beauties:

"Beautiful are its houses, inlaid with turquoise (mosaic),
polished, adorned with stucco (frescoes).
Very wonderful.
What is called a Toltec house
is artistically decorated with drawings
fashioned with perfect artistry throughout."[16]

Ixtlixochitl says that the Toltecs:

". . . did the greatest deeds that are on earth, they were sorcerers, necromancers, witches, astrologers, poets, philosophers and orators . . . and the best painters on earth."[17]

The profusion of frescoes found in the City of the Gods—they are unequalled in Meso-america and perhaps in the world—form one more proof that Teotihuacan was the Toltec capital. (In spite of having been much more thoroughly explored, Tula in the State of Hidalgo has revealed not one centimetre of murals.)

It is unnecessary to insist upon the urgent need for exploration in Teotihuacan*, where every wall is, as it were, a page out of a unique and splendid codex in danger of being lost before its contents have been studied. I myself have more than once been forced to listen passively to a tale of difficulties in the way of detaching frescoes from the old walls that are sometimes dug up during ploughing. "They are so frail, goes the lament, "that many are destroyed before one piece can be rescued for selling...."

These walls crumbling in the peasants' hands hold the key to the spiritual structure of Meso-america.

Fortunately the ceramics, which in Teotihuacan reached the perfection of a great art, also contain many symbols. Innumerable decorative techniques were used, but there are two main types in which religious scenes are shown: fresco and low-relief, called *champ-levé*. The author of the *Annals of Cuauhtitlan* was doubtless referring to the first of these types, more impressively beautiful than the other, when he spoke of the great Quetzalcoatl, King of Tollan:

> "He was a very great craftsman in his objects of earthenware, in which he ate and drank . . . they were painted blue, green, white, yellow and red...."[18]

These are precisely the colours found in Teotihuatecan ceramics painted in fresco. We reiterate that not one single object in this technique has been discovered in Tula-Xicotitlan. The ceramics from the latter site, the so-called *Mazapan*, which some archaeologists consider to have been the prototype of Toltec

* In my Foreword to this book I talk of a season of exploration carried out from October 1955 to February 1956. As we go to press I have just received the good news that the Mexican Department of *Hacienda* has promised me a further grant for continuing this work. L.S.

19 COYOLXAUHQUI, Huitzilopochtli's sister. The symbols carved on her cheeks can be seen in diagramatic form in Figure 63

20 COATLICUE, the mother goddess

ceramics, is composed of plates uniformly decorated with wavy red lines (Fig. 12).

It is thus thanks to the decorations on the ceramics and to the richness of content of the few murals that have been unearthed, that a study of Nahuatl symbolism at its source is possible.

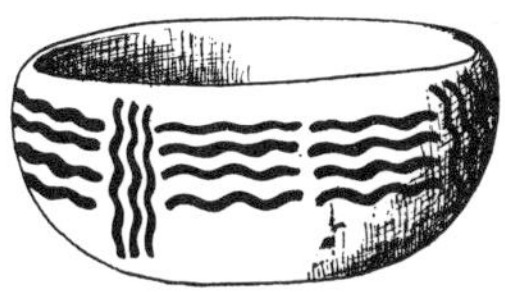

Fig. 12. Ceramic of a kind known as Mazapan, because it was first found at a site bearing that name and situated near the ceremonial centre of Teotihuacan. The type as illustrated is made of a creamy, coffee-coloured clay with red lines. This type is characteristic of Tula-Hidalgo, where great quantities have been found.

V

UNION OF WATER AND FIRE

There is proof that the dynamics of the union of two opposites is at the basis of all creation, spiritual as well as material.

The body "buds and flowers" only when the spirit has been through the fire of sacrifice; in the same way the Earth gives fruit only when it is penetrated by solar heat, transmuted by rain. That is to say, the creative element is not either heat or water alone, but a balance between the two. It is in fact in this dual aspect that the divinity of celestial rain is frequently met with.

Although generally considered to represent only the element water, the god Tlaloc is often closely allied to fire. For example, the Era over which he reigned finally vanished beneath a rain of fire, whereas that which was destroyed by the deluge is ruled over by the goddess of terrestrial water and has no connexion at all with Tlaloc.

The close bond existing between Tlaloc and fire becomes very evident when he assumes his rôle of: "god who inhabits

Fig. 13. Denizens of the Terrestrial Paradise painted in fresco, from Teotihuacan.

Fig. 14. Tlaloc, the Rain God, bearing the Cross of Quetzalcoatl; the Flower of the Sun issues from his mouth. (Teotihuatecan fresco.)

the terrestrial paradise and who gives men the sustenance necessary for their bodily life. . . ."[19] There is a fresco in Teotihuacan which helps us to clarify this point, the far-reaching significance of which will not be fully appreciated until we have advanced more deeply into an analysis of the symbols.

This fresco covers a wall of one of the three excavated palaces. Because the scene depicted is so exactly similar to the Terrestrial Paradise as Sahagún's Aztec informant described it to him, it has been deciphered down to its smallest detail.[20] Besides emphasizing a typical aspect of Meso-american, and particularly of Nahuatl culture—the reverence in which the earliest tradition was held—these scenes are of particular religious interest.

In a previous chapter, when we noted that the dead were not always cremated, we put forward the hypothesis that those who were left without this final purification must have been the uninitiated who had died unredeemed; for their confinement to an earthly habitation, ideal though it may have been, shows how great was the inner abyss that was supposed to separate them from the blessed in heaven.

These paintings are clear indications that the inhabitants of

Fig. 15. The Rain God presiding over the Terrestrial Paradise. The face is conventionalized. The yellow hair (diagonal lines) and the mask's rhomboid eyes are characteristic of the Fire God.

this Eden had not risen beyond the human state (Fig. 13). There are tiny figures with heads and bodies naked. They are in the grip of passions: some are laughing, others weeping. They are taking part in a wild tumult of dances and games, all delightfully expressive but unusual in the City of the Gods, where impenetrability and immobility are the rule.

This charming image of creation is enclosed in a rectangle formed by two serpents intertwined and covered with signs of water and heads of Tlaloc.

The rectangle, the serpent, and the terrestrial water are synonymous with matter, but the heads of Tlaloc bear heavenly hieroglyphs: the quincunx in the form of a cross (a sign certainly connected with fire[21]), and the four-petalled flower of the sun (Fig. 14). The appearance of these fire symbols would not in itself prove that the union of opposites was being represented, if it were not for the more definite proof contained in the scene represented immediately above. Their presence in this context has led many students to equate them with the symbol for water, though such an equation presents special problems which these students have not troubled to solve.

The deity in the centre of the fresco has been identified as Tlaloc (Fig. 15); he is certainly the god who, according to Sahagún, reigns over the Terrestrial Paradise. The mask decor-

Fig. 16. Aquatic signs appearing in Teotihuacan.

ated with teeth, the starfish, and the wavy lines adorning the volutes that issue from his mouth; the open sea-shells he holds in his hands and from which drops of water are spilling, all announce his identity (Fig. 16).

But why do we find in this watery domain the large yellow (fire-coloured) wig which falls over the god's shoulders, and the rhomboid-shaped eyes of his mask, the most usual adornment for the god of fire (Fig. 17)? If we attach these symbols to Tlaloc, we shall deprive the earlier god of his most essential attributes. Luckily for him, there is evidence that prevents such an injustice. Above this complex figure are two borders, one enclosing the signs for water, and the other yellow (!) and dotted with butterflies. This brilliant insect *is* fire. We shall not interrupt our argument to study instances in which the symbolism is obvious, but shall merely remark that in the codices he represents flame. It is clear that this vision of Earth as Paradise is based on the concept of the dynamic harmony between water and fire.

We find this same concept in another image of Tlaloc painted in fresco on a Teotihuatecan vase (Fig. 18). Besides his characteristic circles that look like a huge pair of goggles, the god bears butterfly motifs, as can be seen if his wings are compared to those of the butterfly in Fig. 19. The fact that there is here a union of opposites and not of purely watery elements is confirmed by the presence of the two bands crossed on the god's breast and forming the hieroglyph *Movement* (*Ollin*).

This idea of opposing forces is constantly present in Nahuatl symbolism. There can, for example, be no other explanation for the extraordinary fact that the image: "of the ancient god and father of all the gods, who is the *god of fire*, is in the pool of water in the midst of the battlements and surrounded by stones like roses. . . ."[22]

And why did the Aztecs build their capital in the place where they found a stone from which flowers sprang, and a fountain where the water was: ". . . very red, almost like blood, which divided into two streams, and from the second of the two the water issued so blue and dense that it was frightening . . .?"[23]

What can these wonders have referred to, other than the doctrine which teaches that matter "buds and flowers" because of the power uniting the opposites? This is made still clearer by

Fig. 17. Huehueteotl, ancient Fire God, the first god known to have existed in Meso-america. (Mexican National Museum.)

the fact that in Aztec art the prickly pear, fruit of the miraculous stone, is given the shape of a human heart (Fig. 20); and by the fact that two similar streams of water symbolize the "blossoming war" which man must wage in his efforts to obtain freedom.

Led astray by Aztec materialism and perhaps also by an excess of rationalism, archaeologists have frequently followed Seler's lead and supposed the hieroglyph for the "blossoming war" (Fig. 21), the *atl-tlachinolli* (*atl,* water; *tlachinolli,* something that has been burned) to be the symbol not of an interior struggle but of the war men wage against one another externally. Such an interpretation cannot be maintained if the iconography is studied, because this hieroglyph always accompanies the Lord

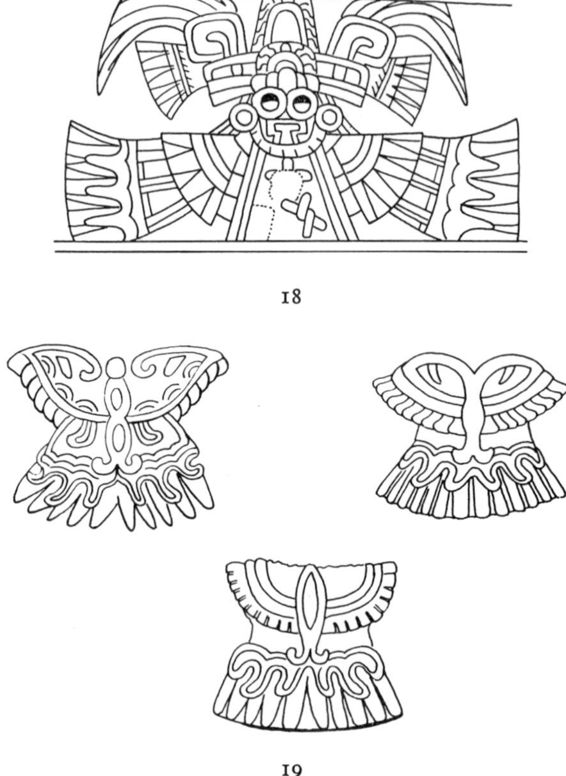

18

19

Fig. 18. God of Rain painted in fresco on a Teotihuatecan vase. He has butterfly wings, and on his breast is the hieroglyph *movement.*

Fig. 19. Teotihuatecan ceramic stylizations of butterflies. (Teotihuatecan Museum.)

of the Dawn, the Star of the Morning, Quetzalcoatl. Figure 22 shows an Aztec representation of Quetzalcoatl bearing as a kind of breastplate the image of the burning water; Figure 23, from a Teotihuatecan fresco, represents the Lord of Dawn struggling against opposing forces: he appears in a ship—that is, on the water—and is encircled by flames. He is armed with the characteristic Nahuatl weapon, an instrument called *atlatl* which is

Fig. 20. Sculptured Aztec monument. (Mexican National Museum.) Below, the River Goddess (Chalchiuhtlicue); from her body springs a prickly pear tree laden with fruit which symbolizes the human heart. Presiding over the scene is the eagle, representing the Sun.

Fig. 21. Hieroglyph of the burning water, two streams uniting, one (enclosed in wavy lines) of water, one of fire.

used for shooting arrows. The motifs in the enclosing borders are essentially the same as those with which the Aztecs later represented the *atl-tlachinolli.*

But is it really necessary, after what the myths have taught us, to prove still once again that the divine spark is freed only when matter is burned up? Quetzalcoatl's message is just this. We have seen how the individual soul of the King of Tollan was freed from his cremated body, and also how the cosmic soul emerged from the ashes of the old man covered with sores. These two narratives show very clearly that the liberating fire is the fire of sacrifice and of penitence; and it is known that the institution of the priesthood had but one purpose: to teach the practices leading to detachment from our earthly condition. It is thus clear that the trophy coveted by the warrior in the "blossoming war" was nothing else but his own soul.

Fig. 22. Aztec monument representing Quetzalcoatl bearing the hieroglyph *burning water*, emblem of the blossoming war. (Compare with fig. 21.)

This spiritual principle is so basic that the Great Temple at Tenochtitlan was dedicated to it: the fact that the gods of rain and celestial fire were placed side by side at the top of the pyramid cannot be seriously interpreted in any other way. The construction of the temple on the site of the fountain from which the blue and red water flowed is also significant, and shows that the gods ruling over it symbolized the mystic formula of "burning water".

This hypothesis is upheld by the presence of statues flanking the stairway (Fig. 24), each carrying a flowering heart in the manner of a standard. We are reminded that, however degenerate they may have become in practice, the rites observed in this sanctury were theoretically destined to offer souls to the sun.

Thus the Great Temple simply reflects the vision which the Aztec oracles longed to contemplate in order that they might lay the foundations of their metropolis: the burning water and the flowering stone, which together make up the two acts of the drama of cosmic union.

Fig. 23. Quetzalcoatl in his aspect of Lord of Dawn (Tlahuizcalpantecuhtli). (Teotihuatecan fresco.)

Fig. 24. The Great Temple of Tenochtitlan as represented in the Codex Florentine. The two idols represent Xochipilli bearing a flowering heart in his hand.

VI

UNION OF HEAVEN AND HELL

As we have seen in the mythology, the Sun also becomes incarnate: every night it is transformed into the Earthly Sun and in the shape of a tiger—symbol of the west and of the Earth's Centre—travels through the subterranean world until it reaches the place from which it rises again into the heavens.

The prowling tiger is one of the most characteristic Nahuatl motifs. There are beautiful examples of it in the frescoes of Teotihuacan; and among the fragments of sculpture preserved in the archaeological museum close to the site are those of tigers' feet in motion. Judging by their size, they must have adorned a very large building. The nightly journey of the Sun corresponds to that of Venus when it goes underground in order to re-emerge as the Morning Star, or that of the King of Tollan when he goes to the redeeming fire. Both these symbolize the movement reuniting opposites. There is one Teotihuatecan fresco which shows this clearly. A tiger and a coyote (wolf-dog), the animal

Fig. 25. Tiger (right) and coyote (left), representing respectively the Sun and Quetzalcoatl in their subterranean pilgrimage. (Teotihuatecan fresco.)

form of Quetzalcoatl, are moving forward in the same direction (Fig. 25). These two creatures are painted on the lower portions of the walls, that is, in the subterranean regions.

The celestial bodies imprisoned in matter are also represented on a page of the *Codex Borbonicus* (Fig. 26). Here the wolf-dog bears the symbols of his illustrious god-man counterpart, and the Sun, in the belly of the Earth Monster, is swathed and bound like a corpse. We recall that one of the dead epochs is that of the Earth-Sun presided over by the tiger.

In the heavens the Sun is an eagle, but he is no more stable in this shape than in the previous one, because at every twilight he is plunged again into darkness. (The sun in the west is called *cuauhtemoc*, or falling eagle, the prophetic name of the last Emperor of the Pre-columbian world.) This reminds us of the Era that vanished beneath the *Rain of fire*, from which only the birds escaped.

The hieroglyph of the burning water symbolizes the struggle of this igneous mass against matter, which constantly threatens to annihilate it. The warlike attitude of certain eagles and tigers in the codices and murals (Figs. 27, 28) no doubt refers to this struggle. We know, too, that the powerful Order of Knights Eagles and Tigers had only one aim, to wage the "blossoming war" (Fig. 29); and all the facts lead us to the conclusion that the civic character this order assumed in Aztec society was a

Fig. 26. The Earth Sun, and Quetzalcoatl in his animal form. (Codex Borbonicus.)

degeneration from the times of ritual initiation which once represented the sacred battle between heaven and earth, between Being and the Void. Certainly in Teotihuacan these knights appear without any trace of profanity (Figs. 30 and 31), having none of the martial aspect so dear to the Aztec conquerors: we have only to place them side by side with a photograph of one of their descendants to realize this (Plate 8). But in spite of its interference in Imperial affairs, this order always undoubtedly kept its religious character. It would be difficult, for instance, to

Fig. 27. Symbolic struggle between eagle and tiger. (Codex Nuttal.)

think of the eagles and tigers carved upon certain Aztec drums (Plate 9) as anything but symbols of the struggle that allows the body to blossom into a soul. The Eagle Knight in the centre of Figure 32 is tense with powerful inner strength and seems rather the apotheosis of the inward soul than a barbarian deity surfeited with blood. It is interesting to note that, although so expressive, this image merely reproduces the geometry of the sign *movement* which is placed at the centre of the drawing, to the sign's right.

Because he belongs equally to the dark abyss and the celestial splendour, man is the meeting ground of opposing principles, which die in isolation when they are removed from it. The plumed serpent, being the image of the consciousness of this creative duality, is the key image in the Nahuatl religion.

The unification of the three worlds is often evoked by means of their symbolic beasts. There is one example of this in an archaeological area hidden in the mountains and difficult to

21 AN IMAGE OF QUETZALCOATL from the Huasteca culture. Mexican National Museum

22 DETAIL OF THE BACK of the sculpture shown in Plate 21

Fig. 28. Solar eagle painted in a Teotihuatecan fresco.

reach even today. This appears to have been the place of secret initiation of the Knights Eagles and Tigers. It is a group of sanctuaries, one of which, carved entirely out of the living rock, forms a circular temple containing the images of cosmic harmony: Heaven, Earth, and Hell. The entrance is composed of two enormous heads of reptiles (Plate 10), and beautiful sculptures of eagles and tigers preside over the interior (Plate 11). This same threefold motif, allied to the symbolism of Quetzalcoatl, is treated with wonderful richness of invention in the ceramics and frescoes of the City of the Gods (Figs. 33, 34), and also in the codices of later epochs (Fig. 35).

The Tree of Life is another symbol for this same unity.

Figure 20 shows a Tree of Life carved on an Aztec monument. Matter is represented by the Goddess of terrestrial water; heaven by the Solar Eagle sounding the hymn of the burning water. Their union is effected by means of a nopal cactus laden with hearts in flower. Alfonso Caso has shown that this is the emblem of Tenochtitlan.[24] This image illustrating the wonders that took place at the site of the future capital of the Empire represents a synthesis of the doctrine of Quetzalcoatl.

In other symbolic terms the Mayan Tree (Plate 12) represents the same synthesis. At its base is the Earth Monster, whose headdress bears the signs of death and resurrection. Then comes man, his feet treading on matter and his head rising upward to the east like the Morning Star. He is pierced by the cosmic hub, at whose summit is the Sun Bird. Evidently we are in the presence of a scene of initiation into the spiritual life, the only one that allows communication among the three worlds.

Fig. 29. Teotihuatecan ceramic figure representing an Eagle Knight. (Mexican National Museum.)

Fig. 30. A Knight Eagle painted in a Teotihuatecan fresco.

The Tree of the Codex Borgia (Fig. 36) is still more explicit. Below is matter in the form of death; above, the Sun. The space uniting them is entirely occupied by a great circle enclosing concentric lines which look like a whirlwind and symbolize the dynamics of the reconciliation between opposites. The two anthropomorphic sacrificial knives flanking the base of the tree-trunk emphasize the religious significance of the picture. In the west, to the left of the tree, is Quetzalcoatl; in the east Xochipilli, Lord of Flowers, who is also, as we shall see, Patron of Souls and represents the freed spirit. The whirlwind separating them expresses the circular creative movement of the Fifth Sun: the descending movement of Quetzalcoatl into Hell, and the ascent of Xochipilli to heaven. Each of the gods carries in his hand a shinbone from which a red stream gushes earthward. It reminds us of how Quetzalcoatl saved man from death. The whole picture represents the geometry of the sign *Movement*.

All these images confirm the myths and merely underline the essential rôle of man in the ordering of cosmic harmony. Such harmony is brought about only through constant spiritual regeneration.

Another hieroglyph contains very beautiful proof of the importance human behaviour has for Creation as a whole. This is the split tree symbolizing the garden, Tamoanchan: ". . . the house of descent, place of birth, mystic west where gods and men originated. . . ."[25] Because the home of the human race is represented by a tree, some tribes, as for example the Mixtecas (a tribe which inherited the Nahuatl culture and passed it on to the nomads who arrived late upon the Mexican plateau) are called "descendants of the trees", and express their origin in the form of a man jumping out of a split tree-trunk (Fig. 37). Since the tree is a kind of cosmic pillar, the split from which the indi-

Fig. 31. A Knight Tiger. Drawing made from a Teotihuatecan fresco discovered by the author in Teotihuacan in February 1956.

Fig. 32. Aztec wood carving. The eagle (left) and the tiger (right) represent the blossoming war achieved by the union of two contraries. The central figure represents the sun in the creative attitude of *movement*.

vidual emerges shows birth to be a separation, a theft; and that unity and movement are re-established only if the incarnate particle can rise upward again to God.

VII

THE HEART AND PENITENCE

The heart is the place of union where the luminous consciousness is made. This organ represents the kernel of religious thought, not only because it occupies a central position in the body, and not only because of the feelings of love which it evokes—feelings that certainly play a vital rôle in Quetzalcoatl's message—but chiefly because of its dynamic function in the body. What more perfect symbol could be found for the creative, liberating movement, than this vibrating piece of flesh whose pulsation at every moment rescues corporeal matter from the inertia and decomposition that lurks in ambush?

Nahuatl symbolism contains an infinite variety of images to represent the heart. Two of these are to be found in Teotihuacan. One, which appears close to the mouth of the tiger and the

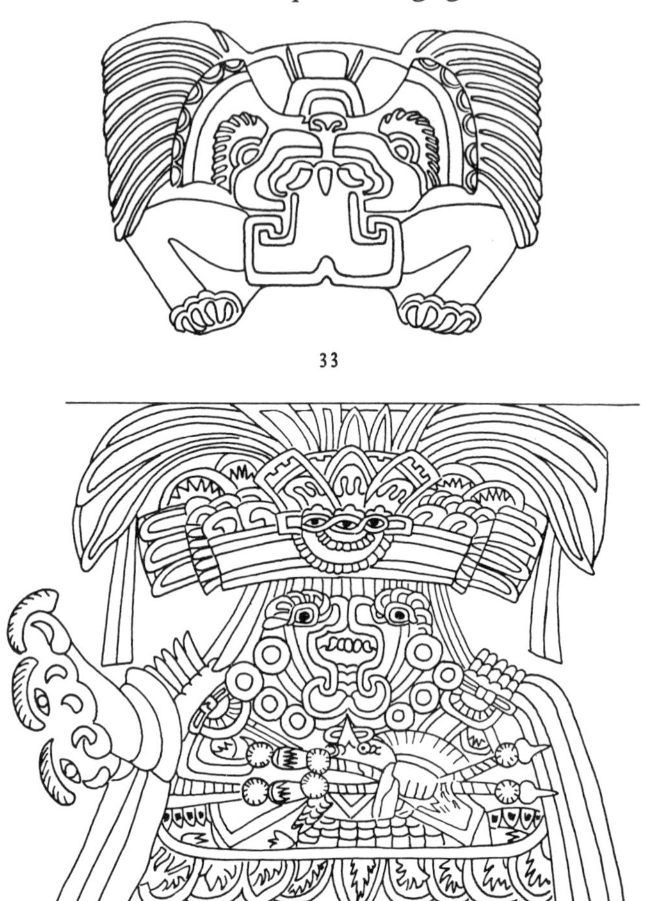

Fig. 33. Tiger-Bird-Serpent carved on a Teotihuatecan vase.

Fig. 34. Tiger-Bird-Serpent, symbolizing the reintegration of the three cosmic forces. (Teotihuatecan fresco.)

coyote in Figure 25, represents a horizontal cross-section at the base of the aorta. The three stylized cavities are expressed in the form of spirals, representing the unifying movement. The connexion of this motif with the Earth Sun, Quetzalcoatl's double,

Fig. 35. Reuniting of the diverse cosmic levels, as shown in the Codex Nuttal.

and the Sun Eagle (Fig. 38), which it seems to be feeding, leaves no doubt as to its identity. The other motif is a horizontal cross-section, also at the base of the aorta (it becomes a kind of central eye (Fig. 39), effected by a transverse cut). If we compare it with a cross-section taken from a modern medical text-book (Fig. 40), we can easily see that this motif, which appears frequently in Teotihuacan paintings, is not in any sense arbitrary. Observe, for instance, how it is shown on the headdress of the tiger-bird-serpent of Figure 34.

We have also various times noted that human existence must reach out to transcend the world of forms that conceal the ultimate reality. This reality lives in the heart, and it is necessary to force the heart to set it free at whatever cost; that is the supreme aim of the "blossoming war". Thus to reach one's heart, to possess oneself of it, means to penetrate into spiritual life. The operation is extremely painful, and that is why the heart is always represented as wounded, and why the drops of blood issuing from it are so significant that they alone are a sufficient symbol for it (Fig. 73).

The only weapon powerful enough to pierce matter is puri-

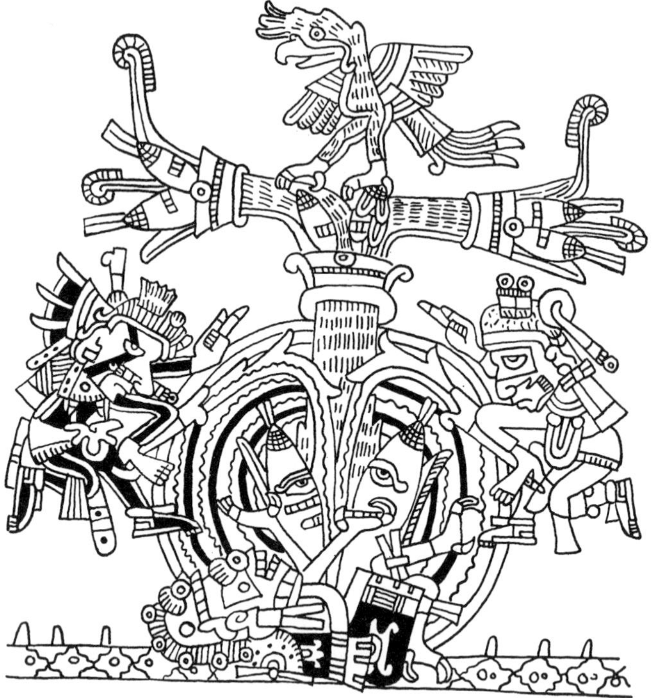

Fig. 36. Tree of Life from the Codex Borgia. Heaven above, Earth below. Quetzalcoatl on the left, Xochipilli on the right, evoke the unifying movement, first of descent and then of ascent.

fication, and so the heart is frequently associated with images of penitence. In Teotihuacan it is usually the sacrificial knife that plays this rôle. A representation of this instrument (Fig. 41), recalling the ceaseless search for spirituality which conscious man must undertake, decorates the freize surrounding an entire *patio* of one of the excavated palaces, and often appears together with a heart, as represented, for instance, in Figure 42.

In Figure 42 we witness the dissection of a heart so that the divine seed enclosed in it may germinate: this is the very moment of the unfolding of the mystic flower, and we find the same motif in the codices of later periods (Fig. 43).

Fig. 37. Symbol for *Tamoanchan,* mankind's native country. (Codex Vindobonensis.)

The symbol of penitence clearly places this individual activity within a cosmic plan. Let us analyse its content. In Figure 44 the two sacrificial knives are stuck into the cactus taking the place ". . . of the lump of plaited straw or hay into which the maguey cactus spikes are driven after they are stained with the blood of self-sacrifice."[26]

The cactus flower and the precious stones that crown it suggest the blood of the offering. The outer wavy band, similar to that in Figure 45, symbolizes fire (we shall meet it again surrounding a Teotihuatecan solar eagle), that is, the luminous energy created by sacrifice. This energy in turn makes possible the universal activity here represented by the rectangles. In fact

Fig. 38. Solar Eagle bearing a human heart in his beak. (Sculpture from a building in Tula-Hidalgo.)

we are faced with a hieroglyph of the *Sun of Movement* (*Ollin*), whose dynamic centre is penitence. In Figure 45 it is the Morning Star that emerges from the sacrificial fire and which by its inevitable ascent suggests the same idea. We should bear in mind that penitence is always symbolized by fiery symbols. The most frequent are a simple volute such as we see by the Lord of Dawn (Fig. 23) and covering the top part of Quetzalcoatl's mace in Teotihuacan (Fig. 52), and also in Quetzalcoatl's hand in the Codex Borbonicus (Fig. 46); and a double volute forming a more or less perfect S (Figs. 55, 61). The double volute is a motif dear to the hearts of Aztec potters.

All this suggests that the materialistic period when the heart was physically laid bare for sacrifice must have been only the end-result of a high, holy and powerful concept. Muñoz Camargo gives a precise detail by which we can penetrate to the inner meaning of these terrible offerings, and which is more explicit than any lengthy dissertation:

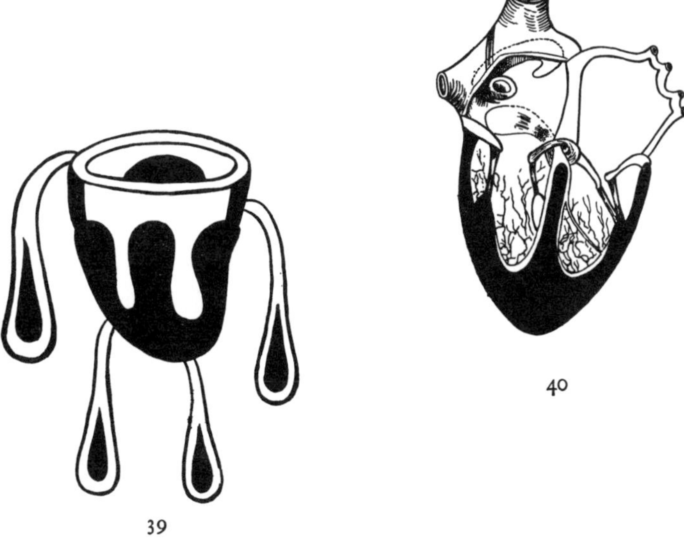

Fig. 39. The human heart as represented in Teotihuacan.

Fig. 40. Cross-section of a human heart. From a medical textbook. A horizontal section taken through the aorta produces a picture identical with the Teotihuatecan heart.

Fig. 41. Obsidian sacrificial knives as shown in a Teotihuatecan fresco.

> "... one who had been a priest of the devil told me ... that when they tore the heart from the entrails and side of the wretched victim, the strength with which it pulsated and quivered was so great that they used to lift it three or four times from the ground until the heart had grown cold...."[27]

Like the most ardent prayer, this heart so madly beating is an expression of man's mystic will to rise upward to God.

Fig. 42. The Lord of Dawn splitting open a human heart.

NOTES

1. Ignacio Marquina, *Arquitectura Prehispanica*, Instituto Nacional de Antropología e Historia, Mexico, 1951.
2. Sylvanus G. Morley, *La Civilización Maya*, Fondo de Cultura Economica, Mexico, 1947 (*Ancient Maya,* Oxford, 1947).
3. Alfonso Caso, *Calendario y Escritura de los antiguos culturas de Monte Albán*, Mexico, 1947.
4. Mapa Quinatzin, *Anales del Museo Nacional*, Epoca I, Mexico, 1886.
5. Sahagún, op. cit., Vol. I, p. 12.

6. Laurette Sejourné, *Tula, la Supuesta Capital de los Toltecas*, Cuadernos Americanos, Mexico, January 1954.
7. The reports on these excavations were submitted by the archaeologist Jorge Acosta. They have not been published entire, and are to be found in the library of the Mexican National Institute of Anthropology and History.
8. Because of the scarcity of material dug up in Tula-Hidalgo—a really extraordinary state of affairs in Meso-america—the Mexican National Museum contains no single room devoted to Toltec culture (which it is supposed to represent), although most outlying archaeological centres have sections all to themselves. This same lack explains a similar gap in the Mexican Art Exhibition of 1952–1953, which caused so much interest when it toured Europe.
9. Sahagún, op. cit., Vol. II, p. 309.
10. All the data concerning the architecture, the placing of the buildings and the orientation of Teotihuacan are taken from the admirable study made by the architect Ignacio Marquina in this archaeological zone between 1917 and 1920 and described in his book already quoted.
11. It is interesting to note that until the very end Nahuatl civilization preserved the custom of surrounding its temples with representations of serpents. Among the few remains found at the pyramid of the Sun, there are two fragments of reptiles from a base moulding. These leave no doubt that the pyramid conformed to this rule (Plate 6).

Fig. 43. Images of pierced hearts, as represented in the Codex Borgia.

Fig. 44. Hieroglyph *movement*. At its centre the emblem of penitence; two sacrificial knives buried in a cactus and encircled with a nimbus. (Teotihuatecan fresco.)

12. Because of the name given to the avenue, the hillocks bordering it were for many years thought to conceal tombs of great lords. Excavation showed this to be false, which is not surprising since the practice of cremating bodies corresponded to a central idea in Quetzalcoatl's doctrine.
13. According to the calculations of the technical workers in the Mexican National Institute of Anthropology and History, less than one-tenth of the whole of Teotihuacan has so far been uncovered.
14. Alfonso Caso, *El Pueblo del Sol*, Fondo de Cultura Economica, Mexico, 1953, p. 21.
15. The art of sculpture flourished during the period of Teotihuacan II, when the ritual centre was built. Painting, on the other hand, flourished in Teotihuacan III, the period to which these palaces belong.
16. *Una Elegía Tolteca*, p. 6. Publication of the Alexander Humbolt Mexican-German Society, Mexico, 1941 (taken from the Madrid Manuscript of Sahagún, Palace Library, and copied by Seler, 1891).
17. Ixtlixochitl, op. cit., Vol. II, p. 40.
18. *Anales de Cuauhtitlan*, op. cit., p. 8.
19. Sahagún, op. cit., Vol. I, p. 22.
20. Alfonso Caso, *El paraíso terrenal en Teotihuacan*, Caudernos Americanos, Mexico, No. 6, 1942.

Fig. 45. Emblem of penitence on an Aztec monument. (Mexican National Museum.)

21. Sahagún specifies that this god "... held in his left hand a shield with five green jewels arranged in the shape of a cross ..." Op. cit., Vol. I, p. 39.
22. Sahagún, op. cit., Vol. I, p. 485.
23. *Códice Ramirez.*
24. Alfonso Caso, *El Teocalli de la Guerra Sagrada,* Talleres Gráficos de la Nación, Mexico, 1927, p. 54.
25. Eduard Seler, op. cit., p. 220.
26. Alfonso Caso, *El Teocalli de la Guerra Sagrada,* op. cit., p. 52.
27. Muñoz Camargo, op. cit.

PART IV
The Nahuatl Gods

I

THE FREE SPIRITS

OUR DIFFICULTY IN UNDERSTANDING the Pre-columbian world lies less in the fact that these symbols are obscure, than in our own lack of a religious sense. Belonging to a civilization whose activities are measured by external fact, in terms of events taking place only in the temporal universe, it is not easy for us to understand motives dictated by the will to rise out of such an existence, to reach beyond our terrestrial condition.

Being representatives of this ideal, the gods are spirits freed for ever from time and dividedness; therefore all that means life to us—expression, personality, movement in time—is prescribed from their images; and their forms, far from being ends in themselves, are hieroglyphs for concepts whose meaning is highly speculative. The meanest of the divine Nahuatl works should be compared to some symbolic whole, such as a cathedral, rather than to a painting or a sculpture. It is therefore natural that these masterpieces should leave us indifferent till we are able to discern the meaning of their language. Look at Figure 34. It is obvious that at first sight this must appear only an utter extravagance, but if we know that this image speaks with absolute precision of the cosmic unity, then perhaps our first impression will change into admiration for the perfect ordering, the equilibrium, and the sobriety of the composition.

This aspiration toward the divine throws light on one characteristic of Meso-american culture: the importance of masks and feathered ornaments. It is understandable that once certain high degrees of consciousness are reached, one would wish to clothe

Fig. 46. Quetzalcoatl bearing in his hand a volute which is the symbol of penitence. (Codex Borbonicus.)

the human figure in holy dignity. We may even wonder whether the headdresses which give expression to the dramatic metamorphosis of the serpent of the earth into the plumed serpent are not part of an attempt to convert the body into a hieroglyph for the mystic formula: only thus uplifted does the heart attain to its true centre.

A passage from the *Annals of Cuauhtitlan* reveals the symbolism of these adornments. It is said that when the demons had given Quetzalcoatl a body, the latter contemplated himself with terror and declared that he would never consent to showing himself in such a form. In order to remedy this lamentable state of affairs, Coyotlinahuatl (the double coyote) suggested:

> "Son of mine, I say that thou shouldst go out so that thy vassals might see thee; and I shall adorn thee that they may see thee. . . ."[1]

and he immediately set to work:

"... he made him first a dress of quetzal feathers
that crossed him from the shoulder to the waist.
Then he made him his turquoise mask,
and took red dye, with which he reddened his lips,
took yellow dye, with which he made little squares on
his forehead,
then he drew in his teeth as if they were serpent's,
and made his wig and his beard of blue feathers
and of red guacamaya feathers, and arranged them very
well,
letting them fall down the back: and when all that
finery was made, he gave Quetzalcoatl the mirror.
When he looked at himself, he saw he was very beautiful,
and it was then
that Quetzalcoatl at once left his retreat
where he had been at watch and prayer...."[2]

Evidently these ornaments, that had the power of ridding him of the horror his body inspired, symbolize a superhuman state. That is why they appear in Teotihuatecan images, and it is worth noting how closely the latter, wig and all, correspond to the mythical description. Sahagún, moreover, states[3] that among the subjects of the king of Tollan were the inventors of the art of featherwork, called *amantecas*, whose presiding divinity was the very one who in the parable dressed Quetzalcoatl as a god. We know that the double coyote (Coyotlinahuatl) represents Quetzalcoatl in his subterranean pilgrimage (Fig. 25); thus the feathers that cover him mark his entry into the light of the spiritual world. More precisely, Sahagún states that these *amantecas*[4] lived in a district called Amantla (today San Miguel Amantla, a suburb of Mexico City), whose archaeological remains, as we have ourselves verified during excavations[5] are of the purest Teotihuatecan style.

We should add here that in spite of their almost exclusive preoccupation with the divine, the artists of the City of the Gods were unequalled in their talent for representing the things of this world, which they considered merely as reflections of the

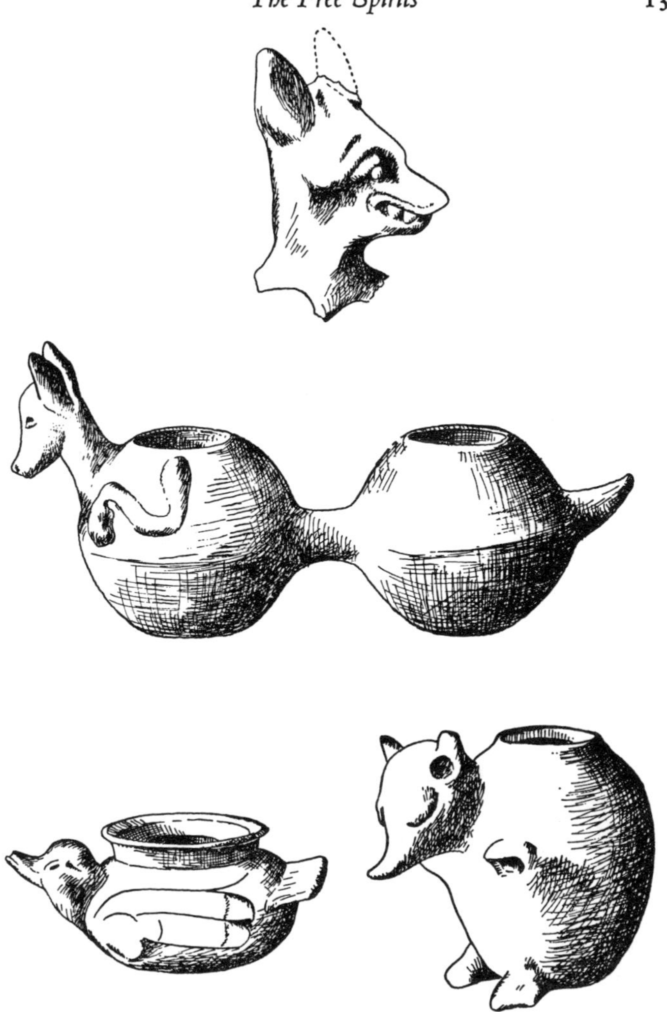

Fig. 47. Animal representations showing how sensitively the Teotihuatecan artists could render living creatures.

other. Certainly the figurines (Plate 13), the dolls (Plate 14), and the animals (Fig. 47) found at this site are among the most lively in Meso-america. The animation of these little figures and the bold charm of the tiny animals reveal a gift of observation

Fig. 48. Teotihuatecan Lord of Earth. (Sculptured vase, Mexican National Museum.)

and a human sympathy from which irony is not altogether absent. Also from Teotihuacan come the beautiful masks that are so full of individuality (Plate 15).

Born of the revelation that the spirit redeems us from the Void, the Nahuatl religion at first devoted itself entirely to exalting this miracle. Therefore the earth, thought of only as a destructive force, scarcely appears in Teotihuacan: the rare representation of the unplumed serpents, which are always found together with contradictory elements, suggest germination. Out of the hundreds of motifs that have been studied, skeletons appear in not more than ten or twelve; and although they were doubtless, like everything else in this symbology, created here, the terrifying Aztec goddesses play only a minor rôle. The reason is that matter is considered in its creative aspect, that is, in movement, as an incarnation of a divine particle proceeding toward the conquest of full consciousness. It is true that there exists a Lord of Earth (Tlatecuhtli) conceived of as: ". . . a

Fig. 49. Quetzalcoatl breathing life into a skeleton. In this image we see his creative function as Wind God. (Codex Borgia.)

fantastic frog, its mouth armed with enormous teeth. . . ."[6] (Fig. 48), but the character of this creature is not very clearly defined.

In the shape of the goddess of the waters (Chalchiuhtlicue, Plate 16), close kin to Tlaloc, matter appears gifted with the power of salvation: vapour, freed from the great mass of water rises heavenward only to return once more to earth after having been made fertile by the sun so that it may create life on earth. Doubtless because of her permanent contact with the celestial spheres, the goddess is invested with the high faculty of purifying. It is she who in the baptismal ceremony frees the newborn child from impurity.

II

QUETZALCOATL

Sahagún deals fully with Quetzalcoatl as King of Tollan, but in his book on the gods he merely says:

> "... He who was man, they took for a god, and said that he used to sweep the path of the gods of water, and they predicted this event, for before the waters begin there are great winds and dust, and so they used to say that Quetzalcoatl, god of winds, swept the paths for the rain gods, so that they might come and rain."[7]

At first sight such a task seems too menial for the creator of the universe of man, but if we remember that the newly-born Fifth Sun was launched upon the heavens by the wind, we can understand how such wind must be the spiritual breath that allows of interior birth. The god symbolic of wind brings in his train the laws that subdue matter: he it is who draws opposites together and reconciles them; he converts death into true life, and causes a marvellous reality to flower out of the dark realm of every-day. It is just because he possesses these powers that Quetzalcoatl is considered the supreme magician—he who holds the secret of all enchantments. That is why the day of the week ruled over by this god is dedicated to necromancers and sorcerers of all kinds.[8]

The Codex Borgia (Fig. 49) reminds us of his rôle as performer of miracles: here he is represented holding a skeleton,

Fig. 50. Quetzalcoatl as Wind God. The flowering shinbone in his headdress symbolizes the birth of matter on a spiritual plane. (Codex Magliabeci.)

into which he is breathing life. The result of this magical operation is the heart, which emerges from the skeleton's fleshless sides. Moreover, one of the most usual symbols for Quetzalcoatl is a shinbone in flower (Fig. 50), and in the Codex Magliabeci (p. 61) he is said to be: ". . . son of another god they call Mictlantecuhtli, who is the Lord of the Land of the Dead." This is an obvious allusion to the doctrine which teaches that matter can be redeemed only by itself dying.

The other images of Quetzalcoatl illustrate the different stages in this process. In the drama the wind causes upon earth, he represents man-become-god: in the first act he is mortal man penetrated by the consciousness of his celestial origin and the anguish of his duality; in the second he is the intrepid pilgrim who goes to hell in order to discover the secret of his nature; in the third, master at last of his inner unity, he is transformed into the planet.

By good fortune we are able to follow the unfolding of this Mystery in the paintings of one of the three excavated palaces in Teotihuacan.

Around a harmonious little *patio*, of so polished a white that it glitters in the sun, are three buildings, each with a portico leading into an inner room. The interiors, built of stucco as white as the *patio's*, are elegantly decorated. Along the lower walls runs a continuous red pattern representing the cross-section of a seashell. Perhaps because of the analogy of the shell (Fig. 51) with the human body which, touched by the spirit's breath, can then achieve new power,[9] this motif is the special emblem of Quetzalcoatl.

The walls of the three porticoes are covered with frescoes in two shades of red, all forming part of a single composition: above a lower panel (as in Fig. 25) a repetitive motif is run in

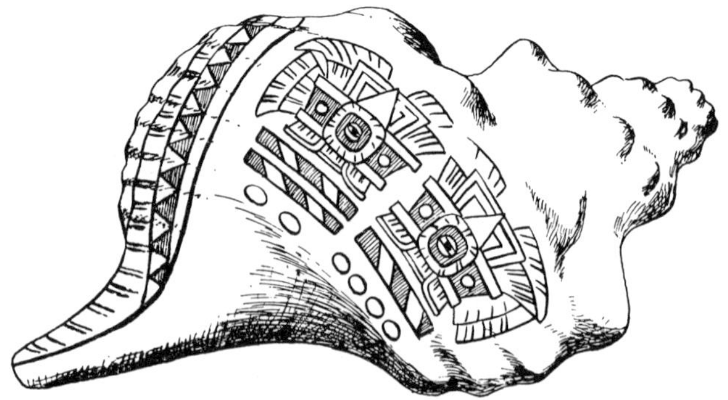

Fig. 51. Teotihuatecan seashell decorated in fresco with two hieroglyphs representing a *cycle* and the numbers 12 and 9. (Mexican National Museum.)

Fig. 52. Quetzalcoatl, from a Teotihuatecan fresco.

such a way as to fill up the remaining space. The design is integrated by a figure standing in the centre of a rhombus formed of entwined plumed serpents.

One of these figures represents the true Quetzal-coatl: the individual concerned only with reaching the interior realm where divinity dwells (Fig. 52). A seashell, probably the symbol of revelation, appears on his breastplate, and his mace is crowned with the symbol of penitence, the only means of advancing along the road to spirituality. The whole composition forms a quincunx with the man-god at the centre, repeating the point of union of the reptiles, the hieroglyph *movement*.

A second portico is presided over by the Lord of Dawn (Tlahuizcalpentecuhtli) (Fig. 53), wearing the black mask of the starry gods and carrying the arrows gathered in the kingdom

Fig. 53. Lord of Dawn, from a Teotihuatecan fresco.

of the dead. Like the other, this figure forms the central point of a quincunx, but in this case the entwined serpents are replaced by an ascending solar eagle bearing the emblem of the cycle of time and surrounded by a halo. It is a vision of wholeness, and marks the completion of the stages of transformation of the serpent into light. The arrows, special sign of this celestial warrior, must represent the interior lightning which reveals the existence of a state of holiness. In the Codex Borgia (Fig. 54) the function of this weapon is illustrated by a wounded reptile from which springs the flowering blood of sacrifice—detachment from the substance of the flesh being an essential requisite for the attainment of a soul. From his mouth emerges the Morning Star: volutes of fire in which are embedded the eyes that symbolize starlight. As we see, this image is found superimposed upon that of the god of wind (characterized by a mask shaped like a bird's beak), and the similarity of their functions shows that the Lord of Dawn is finally reabsorbed into the god who initiates the spiritual adventure, of which he is himself the climax.

The pilgrim into hell, humble and covered with sores, represents the stage separating the revelation from the transfiguration (Fig. 55). He has no right to a place in the beautiful portico, but is found on the pillars of a narrow passage at a lower level than the building. So at these fearful depths the man-god, alone among the shadows, is merely a naked creature filled with panic because he has suddenly lost faith in the creative act. We recall

Fig. 54. The reptile superimposed on the Wind God symbolizes man pierced by the luminous arrow of consciousness. (Codex Borgia.)

how he lamented having lost all in his precipitous flight.[10]

It is probable that the King of Tollan's anguish refers to this trial, the severest of all, wherein, after the death of the things of this world, and on the threshold of a reality still hidden from him, he seems to have become miserably shipwrecked on the shores of the Void.

But he has scarcely touched the depths of his own non-existence, when the shadows open and the pile of broken bones he carries to the light of day revive into new life. From immersion in this higher consciousness in which his own is dissolved, Quetzalcoatl emerges armed with the arrows that allow him, transformed now into the Lord of Dawn, "to shoot his thunderbolts"; they will reveal to human-kind the salvation each individual can try to achieve for himself.

It would seem, then, that Xolotl, who has the thankless task of confronting the ultimate reality, is the chrysalis born of the entrails of the penitent, of the future Star of the Morning. The image of the chrysalis is not in any way arbitrary. This figure (Fig. 56) is always depicted as shapeless, like a larva; moreover the butterfly, symbol of fire, is one of the emblems of the soul. The *Annals of Cuauhtitlan* state that:

> ". . . they say that when Quetzalcoatl died he was not seen for four days, because then he went to dwell among the dead; and that also in four days he was furnished with arrows; so that in eight days there appeared the great star called Quetzalcoatl."[11]

This means to say that Xolotl, personifying the period during which Venus, vanishing out of the western sky and remaining invisible until it appears once again in the east, is simply the seed of the spirit enclosed in matter, the dark region of death. The number 8 (a bar and three points), seen in Figure 55, reminds us of these days spent in the infernal regions. Once more we see how closely the murals of Teotihuacan correspond to the myth.

Fig. 55. Xolotl: the larval form assumed by Quetzalcoatl in the Land of the Dead. (Teotihuatecan fresco.)

III

XOCHIPILLI, LORD OF SOULS

Quetzalcoatl is responsible for the movement which, arising in the land of incarnation (the west) and passing through the centre of matter, proceeds to the kingdom of the spirit. And it is the representative of souls who symbolizes the movement of ascension from the eastern horizon.

Four years after their deaths, according to the Aztecs, the souls of warriors:

> "become various kinds of feathered birds, rich and colourful",[12]

and in this form they go to meet the new-born Sun, to escort him to the zenith.

The soul is represented not only by the bird, but also by the butterfly and the flower. Thus at the beginning of the discourse announcing to the dead man his entry into the other world, the butterfly is mentioned as being among the inhabitants of heaven:

> "Wake, for now it begins to grow light, now is the dawn, for now the yellow-feathered birds begin to sing, and the many-coloured birds go flying."[13]

The texts always use the flower in an entirely spiritual sense, and we have already seen that the aim of the religious colleges was to cause the flower of the body to bloom: this flower can be no other than the soul. The association of the flower with the sun is also evident. One of the hieroglyphs for the sun is a four-petalled flower, and the feasts of the ninth month, dedicated to Huitzilopochtli, were entirely given over to flower offerings. Sahagún refers to this:

> ". . . Two days before the feast all the people poured out into the meadows and cornfields in search of flowers of all kinds, both of woodland and field . . . another day very early was the feast of Huitzilopochtli; the priests offered to this idol flowers, incense and food, and adorned it with

Fig. 56. Images of Xolotl expressing the dynamic feeling of penitence. The hieroglyph *movement* to the right of the scene is also suggested in the composition of the two figures. (Codex Borgia.)

> wreaths and garlands of flowers; having made this statue of Huitzilopochtli out of flowers, and having presented him with many, very cunningly made and very sweet-scented, they did the same to all the statues of all the other gods and all the temples, and then in all the Lords' and headmen's houses they adorned the idols each one possessed with flowers, and offered them other flowers which they placed before them, and all the common folk did the same in their houses."[14]

It is surely not by chance that the only monthly ritual without human sacrifice should have been dedicated to the bloodthirsty

Fig. 57. Xochipilli, Lord of Flowers. Teotihuatecan vase painted in fresco. (Collection Diego Rivera.)

Huitzilopochtli. Evidently what are being so generously offered to the sun are souls, and this is one of the rare cases in which the original symbolism suffered no later degeneration into materialism.

As the bird, the butterfly, and the flower are the symbols for one particular divinity, it is clear that the Lord of Flowers, Xochipilli, must be the personification of the soul. He it is who "has the power of giving flowers", and, since he is not a god of vegetation, the flowers must be spiritual. There are many other proofs that this is so. Firstly he was: ". . . more particularly god of those who dwelt in the houses of the Lords or in the palaces of the headmen"[15] and this is quite natural, because only the Nobles were permitted to be initiated into the mysteries which enabled them to be gathered back into heaven. Then too, severe sexual abstinence was imposed during his feast, together with rigorous fasts and self-sacrifice; some ". . . anointing their ears with blood before him; others pierced their tongues with maguey thorns, and through the hole passed many thin threads, spilling blood. . . ."[16] All this would be unexpected, to say the least, if Xochipilli were the god of games and diversions, as has

Fig. 58. Xochipilli, Lord of Flowers. Teotihuatecan vase painted in fresco. (Teotihuatecan Museum.)

been supposed; but it becomes understandable if he is Patron of Souls. Finally it is he who bears the standard of the "blossoming heart" (Fig. 24) at the foot of the stairs of the Great Temple of Tenochtitlan, and who appears in the Codex Borgia to the east of the Cosmic Tree (Fig. 36).

We possess classic representations of this god on two Teotihuatecan vases painted in fresco (Figs. 57, 58). Because their component shapes have only a hieroglyphic value, and because every outward expression represented to the mystics of the City of the Gods the boundaries of the human prison, a first glance at these figures impresses us only because of their exact symmetry and careful arrangement. Nevertheless an attentive eye will soon discover, beneath the extreme austerity of the exterior, the glorious signs of the resurrection they herald; the brilliant shimmering of wings and petals in the dawn evoke the miracle of spiritual light blossoming from darkest night.

The face of the Lord of Flowers is painted red, and Sahagún explains this fact:

> ". . . the image of this god was like a naked man who has been flayed."[17]

Does not this flaying remind us of the splitting open of matter which encloses the seed of life? And could we ask for a more robust metaphor to describe the being made of light that is in us, and its painful ascent out of terrestrial loneliness, than this burning image of a flayed creature?

More realistic than their predecessors, the Aztecs endowed Xochipilli with expression, and in doing so created their most moving work of art (Plate 17). The symbolism is the same as that of the god's Teotihuatecan ancestor, but here the ecstasy of the soul in communion with the great unity is expressed with a pathetic fervour which holds in suspense the body and the face torn of its flesh.

IV

XIPE TOTEC, LORD OF LIBERATION

Having, thanks to Xochipilli, discovered that the body's skin symbolizes matter, which man must sacrifice to achieve salvation, we now know that the penitential act was regarded as a progressive flaying of the body.

This fact at once reveals to us the meaning of the most hermetic of all Nahuatl divinities: Xipe Totec, so-called Lord of Flaying. His attributes and functions, though apparently contradictory, are generally agreed to be those of the god of liberation (Plate 18).

Deceived by the analogy of the skin shed with each cyclic re-creation of nature, investigators have called Xipe God of Spring, in spite of the fact that, like Xochipilli, he belongs to

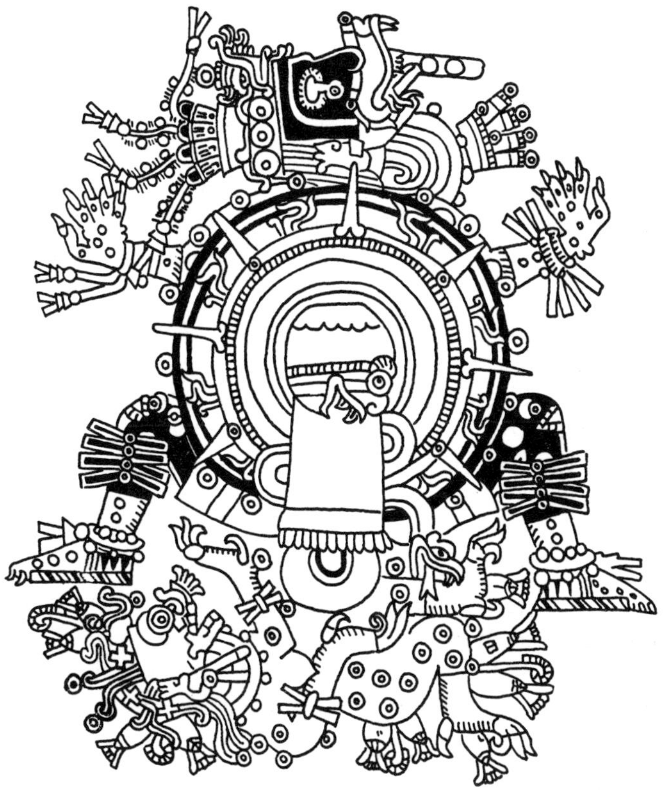

Fig. 59. The penitent Xolotl lighting the sun. (Codex Borgia.)

the region of the new-born sun, in the opposite quarter from that of terrestrial birth. Moreover Sahagún says nothing that could be interpreted as confirming these investigators' views. He merely tells us that:

> ". . . they attribute to this god the following illnesses: firstly smallpox, also the boils that occur on the body, and the scabs, also eye diseases."[18]

These illnesses, while they seem odd in a god of vegetation, perfectly match the symbolism of penitence. In fact if we remember that the Fifth Sun was born of a body covered with sores, we have another proof that the illnesses are signs announcing that what has held the spirit in bondage is being annihilated. The reference to diseases of the eyes is perhaps explained by a strange image constantly appearing in Meso-american iconography: an eye bursting, or depicted outside its socket. Together with tumours, the burst eye is one of Xolotl's most constant characteristics (Fig. 56). It is probably a symbol for the sacrifice of external sight which is necessary for the attainment of internal illumination and the inner vision. Be this as it may, it is extremely significant that the functions Sahagún's informants attribute to Xipe are those of the supreme penitent, the lamed hero of the "blossoming war". It should be noted that Xolotl is the chrysalis of the universal as well as of the individual soul. He is the sore-ridden god of the myth, who gives birth to the Sun (Fig. 59).

Among the Aztecs the Penitent seems clearly to duplicate the passion of Quetzalcoatl in the underworld. Naked like Xolotl, he goes through the most severe ritual trials—such as immersing himself in icy water or plunging into the depths of a wood at midnight, when darkness reigns upon earth as in the subterranean world; and with the blood of his tortured limbs:

> "... he anointed his face with a line from the eyebrow to the jawbone."

Xipe (Fig. 60) and Xolotl (Fig. 55) are anointed in the same way.

These in fact are the attributes of a god of liberation as summarized in a hymn to Xipe:

> Thou, drinker in the night,
> Why dost thou insist on praying?
> Don thy disguise,
> Put on thy garment of gold.
>
> Oh, my god, thou precious-jewelled water
> hast descended;
> he hath become transformed, the tall cypress,
> into a quetzal bird;

Fig. 60. Xipe, in a Zapotec ceramic. (Mexican National Museum.)

the serpent of fire
has been transformed into a serpent of quetzal.

The serpent of fire has set me free.
Perhaps I shall vanish,
perhaps I shall vanish and be destroyed, I,
the tender corn shoot.
My heart is green
like a precious jewel,
but I shall yet see the gold
and shall rejoice if the war chief
has matured, if he has been born.

Oh, my god, grant that at least
a few corn shoots

put out fruit in abundance;
thy servant turns his gaze toward thy mountain,
toward thee,
I shall rejoice if something matures first, if I can say
the war chief has been born.

It is easy to see that this is a prayer to the god who has the power of raising man to spirituality, and who is called the "drinker by night" precisely because the sacrifice that will bring this about occurs at night:

> "... They used to draw blood from their ears to offer to the gods, which they always did at midnight."[19]

It is known, moreover, that the garment of gold in which he asks to be clad is that same yellow flayed skin whose acceptance frees him from the encumbrance of matter. This hypothesis is strongly supported by the fact that Tlazolteotl, the goddess specially appointed to carry the sins which the penitents confess to the god Tezcatlipoca, appears, like Xipe, clothed in flayed human skin.

The plant aspiring to become mature is an image of the penitent wishing to be converted into a hero in the holy war. This same symbolism is found in the rituals in honour of Cinteotl, son of the Corn Goddess and deity of the young maize shoot, during which young men publicly swear to beat themselves.[20] Cinteotl is, moreover, so closely allied to Xochipilli that it is sometimes hard to differentiate between them; and this relationship with the Patron of Souls clearly demonstrates the spiritual nature of the symbolism of the plant. According to Lumholtz, the Huicholes, a tribe living in the north-west of present-day Mexico, among whom many Nahuatl beliefs and rituals appear to have survived, say that the priests and sorcerers of past times created the Sun by casting the young son of the Corn Goddess into the fire.[21] Cinteotl is thus the penitent who is transformed into the heart of the universe.

The other metaphors all speak of the same nostalgia for libera-

Fig. 61. Head of the Flayed Lord, Xipe, at the centre of a Cross of Quetzalcoatl. Teotihuatecan vase painted in fresco. (Collection Kurt Stavenhagen.)

tion: the fiery serpent is the individual burning with desire to transcend his terrestrial state.

Xipe's connexion with penitence is confirmed by two Teotihuatecan representations. In the first (Fig. 61) he stands at the centre of Quetzalcoatl's cross of fire, and his head is swathed in yellow bandages of flayed skin; the quincunx and the S complete the motif. In the second (Fig. 62) he carries in his hand a vase in the shape of an eagle's claw, and this symbol may refer to certain specific rituals: before dying the victim sacrificed in the god's name must be placed on the so-called "gladiator's stone" to fight against four Knights Eagles and Tigers. Sahagún has left an extremely vivid picture of this combat:

> ". . . They used to make the captive climb on to the stone, round like a grindstone, and when the captive was upon

the stone one of the priests came to him . . . he was a kind of godfather to those that died there, and he took a rope, which went through the eyelet of the grindstone, and bound his waist with it. Then he gave him his wooden sword, which instead of knives had bird feathers stuck to the edge, and gave him four pine staves with which to defend himself and overthrow his adversary. The prisoner's keeper, leaving him in the aforesaid manner upon the stone, went to his appointed place and from there, as he danced, watched what was happening to his prisoner. Then those that were prepared for the fight began to struggle against the captive one by one.

Some of the captives who were brave used to wear out the four who were fighting, who could not make them surrender; then there would come a fifth, left-handed, who used his left hand instead of his right; he defeated him and took away his arms and threw him to earth; then came he who was called Ioallaoa, and he opened his breast and brought out the heart. Some captives, seeing themselves tied to the stone, grew faint and lost courage, and thus, faint and spiritless, took up their arms, but at once allowed themselves to be defeated, and their hearts were removed upon the stone. Some captives there were who lost consciousness when they found themselves bound to the stone; they threw themselves to earth without taking up any weapon, desiring that they be killed at once, and so they did, throwing them upon their backs on the edge of the stone."[22]

After the victim had been flayed, the owner would share out the morsels among his "superiors, friends and relatives," taking care nevertheless not to taste them himself, because: "the captive's master did not eat the flesh, for he knew it was his own flesh."[23]

It need no longer be emphasized that all these rites represent externalized forms of trials of initiation presided over by the god who, freeing the individual from the limitations of time, opens the doors to the infinite. The symbolism could not be more eloquent: after the union of opposites brought about by the fifth and left-handed knight, the neophyte is relieved (by

Fig. 62. Ceramic sculpture of Xipe, God of Liberation. (Teotihuatecan Museum.) He carries in his hand a vase shaped like an eagle's claw.

flaying) of his earthly clothing and is freed for ever from his body (an act represented by the dismembering of the corpse).

The mystical significance of these rites is emphasized by the behaviour of the owner of the sacrificed prisoner. Not only does he dance, miming the various stages of the combat and death; he also behaves toward the corpse as if it were his own body. This identification suggests that the slave represents the master's body offered to the god, the former being merely a symbol for the latter. The drama thus unfolds on two planes: that of the invisible reality, and that of finite matter, a mere projection of the former. The emphasis which Sahagún places upon the behaviour of the victim is no doubt due to the fact that each gesture had its precise inner equivalent, and because the captive's whole attitude foretold the owner's spiritual destiny. It is obvious that if matter (the slave), instead of showing itself to be still dominated by earthly passions such as attachment to life and fear of death, were to emerge victorious from the struggle, then the soul (the owner) would attain salvation. The offerings must have had to be repeated until the heroism of one of these carnal images announced that the initiate had at last moved to a spiritual plane.

This symbolism is also observable in the sacrifices to the God of Fire. Here the owner, before hurling the slave's body into the purifying fire,

> "... partnered the captive; the two danced as a pair."[24]

The owner seems to have represented the spirit—his face painted red like Xochipilli's and a butterfly made of red parrot feathers for his emblem—and the slave matter. The latter was clad entirely in white (the colour of the terrestrial goddess and of the land of birth).

From all this we can see that it was not supposed to be the poor wretches outside the law who attained to the Sun, but the Lords and Nobles who offered them up as sacrifice. Sahagún states that this is so, and it must have been a natural arrangement in so hieratic a society. We shall return to the theme of this aristocratic partition of heaven. It throws light on the kind of theological speculations that were indulged in for the purpose of placing Nahuatl spirituality at the service of an Empire, and it allows us better to understand the economy which ruled human sacrifice among the Aztecs.

V

HUITZILOPOCHTLI: THE FIFTH SUN

With the help of the souls of the blessed, who escort him to the zenith dancing and singing,[25] the Sun completes his heroic ascension out of the field of the earth's influence. In his mid-day fulness the Sun is personified by Huitzilopochtli, the left-handed god disguised as a humming-bird, symbol of resurrection. (The Aztecs used to say that this bird died during the droughts and was reborn at the beginning of the rainy season.)

Because of his essentially warlike nature and of the fact that he was known to the nomad tribes, it has generally been supposed that Huitzilopochtli is of Aztec origin. But although some of his characteristics may have been invented by the builders of Tenochtitlan, the roots of his symbolism must certainly have sprung from the very heart of Quetzalcoatl's doctrine.

We know that the Fifth Sun appears after four others have come and gone, and that this Fifth Sun is itself destined to be superseded by another. We cannot believe that these myths of solar cataclysms were inspired only by the eternal cosmic renewal manifest in natural cycles. Apart from the fact that Nahuatl religious phenomena, which are so highly spiritual, could never be so simply explained—in terms, that is, that have no inner meaning—there are various indications that the Fifth Sun is the creator of a great and indestructible work: that of freeing creation from duality.

We have seen that a tradition exists, and is spoken of by all the chroniclers, according to which the planets will finally take the place of man upon the earth. The essence of the Nahuatl religion is contained in the revelation of the secret which enables mortals to escape destruction and to resolve the contradiction inherent in their natures by becoming converted into luminous bodies. We can therefore draw the conclusion that the next Era, far from being inimical to them, was painfully prepared for and ardently awaited by the conscious men of the Fifth. This is proved by the fact that the Fifth Era, already foreshadowing one that is to follow, was presided over by a Sun to which a penitent gave birth; and that Huitzilopochtli, image of this Sun, disguised as a bird and with fire as his sign, represented the soul of a combatant in the holy war.[26]

We know, too, that the sign *Movement* peculiar to the Fifth

Sun refers to the operation which rescues matter from inertia. The word *ollin* contains the meaning "earthquake", and *Ollin Tonatiuh*, the name of the Fifth Sun, signifies "Sun of the Earthquake". It seems clear that the inner impulse suggested by earthquakes recalls that other movement which allows the mystic to set free the spiritual germ within him. The myth of the birth of the Fifth Sun, together with representations of the sun rising from the shattered body of Xolotl are sufficient proof. The advent of the planets must occur immediately after terrible earthquakes, and these upheavals of matter are, on the cosmic scale, parallel to those which the penitent suffers in his body. This indicates that at the end of the Fifth Era the earth, gripped by a longing for unity, would give birth to luminous and immortal beings.

Huitzilopochtli is then the fifth left-handed warrior who, in the likeness of the one who vanquished the hero sacrificed to Xipe on the gladiator's stone, is destined to gain the ultimate victory.

But in order to reach this supreme goal, he must transmit to matter the *movement* that will bring it to the knowledge of its own duality and the means of rescue from it. In other words he must turn matter into a combatant in the "blossoming war". That is why he is above all the god of war, he who:

> ". . . hurls upon men the fiery serpent [symbol of purifying penitence], the fiery auger [instrument that makes flame rise from a solid body], that is to say, war, devastating torrent, consuming fire"[27] [devourer of darkness and heaviness].

It is for the same reason that during the wanderings of the nomad tribes Huitzilopochtli intervened only to encourage them to go forward and to punish severely those who fell back on the road. Ancient traditions relate that in the shape of a humming-bird he used to repeat continuously to the migrating Aztecs the words, "Forward, forward!"

The myth of his birth is incomprehensible except in the light of this basic material. He was conceived without sin by the penitent Coatlicue, of whom:

"... it is said that one day while she was sweeping a feathery ball descended upon her like a lump of thread, and she took it and put it in her bosom close to her belly, beneath her petticoats, and after having swept she wished to take hold of it and could not find it, from which they say she became pregnant...."[28]

This miraculous conception had the power of awakening the fury of Coatlicue's four hundred sons and eldest daughter, who swore to kill her to avenge the family honour. But just as the goddess was being attacked Huitzilopochtli emerged fully armed from her entrails, and pursued his brothers till they were exhausted. He killed a great number of them after having beheaded his sister.

As Coatlicue is the Earth Goddess, it is clear that the feathers that allow her to give birth to an immortal symbolize the principle that saves matter from the law of destruction. This myth really duplicates that of the birth of the Fifth Sun in Teotihuacan, with the difference that Xolotl's ulcerous body is here represented by the earth mother, and the Sun rising to heaven (the soul of the penitent) by Huitzilopochtli. There are also a number of indications that, just as the gods who were present at the sacrifice which took place in the first Toltec city, so the brothers who witnessed Coatlicue's parturition are actually the Nahua forebears. In both tales pursuit and death represent precisely the creative meeting of matter with spirit, that is to say, they are dealing with the archetypal image of the dynamic meeting of opposites; and it is probable that the ritual races during the Aztec feasts to the Sun God (which also correspond with the myth) simply echo this meeting.

Coatlicue's daughter also represents matter after the advent of the spirit. Besides the combativeness accompanying the arrival of the new sun into the world, which in itself is revealing, there are iconographic documents which uphold this hypothesis.

In the Mexican National Museum, for instance, there is a monumental head which, since its lower portion is decorated in relief, is supposed to be intact as it was originally carved, and never to have formed part of a body (Plate 19). Thanks to the hieroglyph of the goddess's name on both cheeks—the bell represented by the word "Coyolxauhqui"—Seler had no difficulty in identifying the head as Huitzilopochtli's sister. Moreover, this sculpture undoubtedly contains symbols of fire—for example gold, sign of fire (Fig. 63). In his masterly study of the Aztec Codex known as the *Tonalamatl of Aubin*, the German scholar says that:

> ". . . It seems to me probable enough that this head is intended to represent the goddess Chantico. . . ."[29]

In fact the relation of the head to the fire goddess is indisputable, though Seler, fascinated by the theory of the supremacy of lunar myths, which happened to be in vogue at the time, later tried to convince himself that this figure represented the moon.

But Chantico is also considered to be the earth goddess. Not only does Duran identify her with the mother of Huitzilopochtli, but her second name, Quaxolotl, marks her out as "she of the two heads, she of the divided head." The most specific fact about the mother goddess is precisely that she was decapitated like her daughter, and that two snakeheads emerged from her mutilated neck (Plate 20).

In all three cases the same thing is symbolized: matter after the appearance of Quetzalcoatl's spiritual message; that is, matter touched by divine fire. (It is certainly no accident that Coatlicue received the heavenly feathers while she was doing penance in a temple.) In fact all the documents clearly illustrate the spirituality of the Nahuatl goddesses. Unfortunately we cannot here go into a more detailed analysis of this phenomenon, and would merely point out that these goddesses are constantly associated with ideas of purification, penitence, and the "blossoming war".

In this connexion it is significant that the chief symbol of Chantico, female goddess of fire, is burning water; and that it is this same mystic symbol which appears beneath the severed head of the daughter of the Earth Mother. In actual fact the

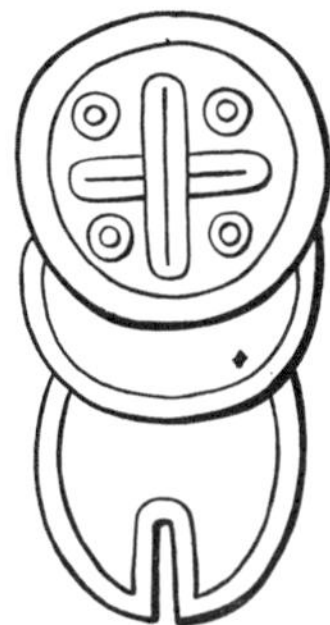

Fig. 63 Hieroglyph for gold carved on the cheeks of Huitzilopochtli's sister.

wound produced by the Sun God's luminous weapon—the fiery serpent with which Huitzilopochtli came into the world—left on the woman's neck the mark of union of opposites. In this sculpture the sign of the burning water has a third element: a sacrificial cord which speaks to matter of the means by which this redeeming union may be attained. As the Mexican art critic, Justino Fernández has clearly observed,[30] the symbolism of Coatlicue bears traces of an undoubtedly superterrestrial nature, among others those of the two serpents upon her head: these are covered with precious jewels, the sign of divinity.

VI

TEZCATLIPOCA: LORD OF THE SMOKING MIRROR

When the Sun leaves the zenith it plunges into the region which is subjected to the law of gravity, and descends into matter accompanied by the western gods. The stages of this journey are marked by successive images of the sun: the humming-bird, sign of its maturity, is replaced first by the descending eagle and then by the tiger.

The symbolism of Tezcatlipoca is very similar to that of the Sun in this fourth quarter of space. The tiger, symbol of the sub-

Fig. 64. Tezcatlipoca, Lord of the Smoking Mirror, in his Tiger form. (Codex Borbonicus.)

terranean depths, is Tezcatlipoca's chief disguise (Fig. 64), his other being the turkey (Fig. 65); and it is likely that this clumsy domestic bird, known as the Great Xolotl (*Hueyxolotl*) is a symbol for the sun exiled upon earth; in other words it is an incarnation of the fallen eagle.

Tezcatlipoca's feast: "which was like Easter and fell close to the Feast of Resurrection . . ."[31] was the most important of all and took place half-way through the fifth month, when the sun first passes through the zenith after the winter solstice. On this occasion Tezcatlipoca, sacrificed in the person of a prisoner, was reborn immediately into the body of another youth, who represented him until he in his turn died at the feast of the following year.

The rituals accompanying these ceremonies were particularly

Fig. 65. Tezcatlipoca in his Turkey form. (Codex Borbonicus.)

moving, because the anonymous horde of sacrificed slaves was here replaced by one solitary individual, whose fate stands out against the cosmic drama in which he had become involved. Because of the rich symbolism of these rituals, we quote Sahagún's lengthy description:

"... At this feast they killed a youth of very docile temperament, whom they had kept for the space of a year in pleasurable activities: they used to say he was the image of Tezcatlipoca. When the youth who had been cherished for one year was killed, they immediately put another in his place to be regaled throughout the next year ... from among all the captives they chose the noblest men ... they took pains they should be the ablest and best-mannered they could find, and with no bodily blemish.

The youth who was reared in order to be killed at this feast, they taught very diligently how to sound the flute well, and fetch and carry the reeds of smoke and the flowers, as was the custom among the headmen and those of the palace. . . . Before this youth was led out to die, they were very careful to teach him all good manners in speech and in greeting those whom he met in the street, and all other good habits; for when he was marked out to die at the feast of this god in that year for which his death had been appointed, all who looked upon him held him in great reverence, and did him great honour, and worshipped him, kissing the earth. . . . Then when this youth was destined to die at the feast of the god, he began to walk through the streets sounding his flute, bearing flowers and reeds of smoke. He was free to walk through the village by night and by day, and eight pages dressed like those of the palace walked with him always. It being known that this youth was to be sacrificed at the feast, then the lord dressed him in curious and precious robes, because now they held him as a god. . . . Twenty days before the feast they changed the clothes in which until then he had made penance . . . and they married him to four virgins, with whom he held converse those twenty days of life remaining to him. . . . The four virgins they gave him for wives had also been much cherished in their upbringing, for that purpose, and they gave them the names of four goddesses. . . . Five days before the feast at which this youth was to be sacrificed, they did him honour as if to a god. The lord stayed alone in his house, and all those of the court followed him, and made him solemn banquets and balls or dances, in very rich garments. . . . The fourth feast being over, they placed him in a canoe covered with an awning, in which the lord used to go abroad, and with him went his wives who consoled him . . . and they sailed to a place . . . where there is a little hill; in that place they left his wives and all the rest of the people . . . only the eight pages accompanied him who had been with him all the year. Then they took him to a small and ill-furnished temple that was beside the road and away from any settlement. . . . Having reached the temple steps he climbed them himself, and on the first step

Fig. 66. Hieroglyph of the smoking mirror; the volutes above the axis—representing a dead man's bone—symbolize the Morning Star.

he broke one of the flutes he had played in the time of his prosperity, on the second he broke another, on the third another, and so broke them all as he climbed the steps. When he had come to the top, to the highest part of the temple, there were the priests who were to kill him, standing in pairs, and they took him and bound his hands and head, lying him on his back upon the block; he that had the stone knife plunged it into his breast with a great thrust, and drawing it forth, put his hand into the incision the knife had made, and pulled out the heart and offered it at once to the sun."[32]

We do not need to make any detailed analysis to see that this is a dramatization of the annual cycle, and that the unblemished youth plays the part of the Sun. It may be that the twenty days preceding his sacrifice symbolize the winter solstice, during which the Sun, sojourning ever longer in the subterranean world, begins to fear for his freedom. This would explain why from that moment the youth changes his divine attributes for those of a warrior: he must beat himself in order not to be conquered by the earth—represented by the four virgins—who try to hold him back. If the winter solstice reproduces on a larger scale the daily drama of light imprisoned by darkness, the prisoner's death must signify his liberation. From which it appears that, as Quetzalcoatl personifies man in the Mystery of the cosmic Passion, death and resurrection, so does Tezcatlipoca personify the Sun; and it is doubtless because of the similarity of the two rôles that the same name is used in both cases, the first being Xolotl, and the second the Great Xolotl. This hypothesis seems, moreover, to be proved by the fact that the ceremonies immediately following upon the death of Tezcatlipoca (Earth Sun) are dedicated to Huitzilpochtli (Sun of the Centre), who seems to rise from the sacrificed body of the Lord of the Smoking Mirror, just as the Morning Star does from that of Quetzalcoatl.

If we set on one side the subordinate accompanying ritual, we see that the second act of the feast of Tezcatlipoca consists in a statue of Huitzilpochtli being solemnly carried to the top of a pyramid. It was usual for the idol to be placed upon stretchers borne by warriors and preceded by a multitude of boys who danced and sang hymns. This scene corresponds word for word with Sahagún's narrative of the Sun's daily ascent in the east, paradise of the heroes of the holy war. The dances that brought the ritual to an end were given a name meaning "they embrace Huitzilopochtli", and must have symbolized the final union of the souls with the Sun, for it is probably the return of these luminous particles to his bosom that enables him to attain to the fullness of his zenith. It is no doubt because of this reintegration that the souls of the warriors are supposed never to succeed in going further than the zenith: so every dawn the Sun was received by other souls, newly blossomed.

It would seem that Tezcatlipoca and Huitzilopochtli are two aspects of the same being. It is therefore understandable that the former representative of the night sky, whose insignia is the starry mitre he carries (Fig. 65), has so often been identified with the latter, the heaven radiant above all.

Contrasts and dualism in fact characterize all Tezcatlipoca's functions. He is Quetzalcoatl's brother and also his enemy; the

Fig. 67. A Mayan with the sign of Venus at the back of his head.

creator and destroyer of the earliest mythical eras; he is god of divine providence, but also of failure and ruin; he is god of

Fig. 68. Mayan Lord of Dawn, with the hieroglyph Venus. (Codex Dresden.)

purity and order, yet he protects sin and foments quarrels; he is the friend of the rich, although he regards slaves—with whose yoke he is frequently represented—as his well-beloved sons; in spite of the fact that he is "considered to be the true god", he is nevertheless sometimes allowed to be captured by men, who brutally impose their will upon him. His invisible omnipresence is "spirit, air, darkness", and his distinguishing sign is a dark and smoking mirror.

His nebulous and shifting character, and also his close connexion with activities of the most profane kind, suggests that Tezcatlipoca, image of the Earth Sun, is really humanity itself, symbolizing the matter in which the Sun becomes incarnate. If this is so, then the many different facets of the god would represent the reflections of this opaque and shifting mass in search of salvation. Only so understood does his chaotic personality become coherent: among the humans living in the Epoch of the Centre there could in fact be nothing more natural than that violence, discord and sin should be present together with the need for harmony and purification.

Omitting technical proofs, which we leave for specialist journals, we shall here confine ourselves to analysing the hiero-

Fig. 69. Hieroglyph of the morning Star as it appears in Zapotec art.

glyph for the name Tezcatlipoca, translated as "smoking mirror" or "smoke that mirrors" (Fig. 66).

The central part is formed of concentric lines similar to those on Xipe's sword; and its outer edge is decorated with feather balls, which are always associated with sacrifice. From its centre emerges a shinbone flanked by volutes in which are incrusted "eyes of light", or stars, and above each volute there is a symbol, which looks like a flame, the symbol of penitence.

The whole composition seems to express the idea of sacrifice; and we in fact know that Tezcatlipoca is closely allied to this basic concept. Not only does he preside over confession, but there exists a legend according to which, when he appears upon earth, whoever has the courage to possess himself of the god's heart can exact from him what is considered the most priceless treasure: a number of the maguey thorns with which self-sacrifice is effected. Besides, his relationship to Quetzalcoatl and to Xipe is proved by a series of documents both iconographic and mythical.

As to the volutes encrusted with stars, they are a sign characteristic of Quetzalcoatl and of his double, Xolotl. With slight

Fig. 70. Venus emerging from a tiger's jaws. Low-relief on an urn pedestal discovered in the entrance to tomb 104, Monte Albán, Oaxaca.

variations they usually form part of the clothing of the former, and they are present in a strange picture of Xolotl being cooked in a kettle (Fig. 56). We know that this personage, whom Seler classifies as god of sacrifice, is the penitent transformed into light, creator both of the Sun and of the planet Venus. The scene we are examining includes no solar sign and must represent the birth of the individual soul. The volutes escaping from the tortured body of Xolotl in fact represent the Morning Star.

This hieroglyph appears frequently in all Meso-american cultures and was perpetuated by the Aztecs. Unfortunately we have not yet found a single example of it in Teotihuacan, but it does appear in various Mayan low-reliefs of the Old Empire (Fig. 67) and also in their painted books (Fig. 68). Students of Mayan civilization have for long associated it with Venus. Among the Zapotecs (Fig. 69), where it is of paramount importance, it is found integrated into a complete pattern whose meaning can easily be deciphered (Fig. 70). The transparent volutes merging from a tiger's jaws clearly reveal the meaning of light engendered by darkness. From a later cultural era we have a very beautiful Huastecan statue of Quetzalcoatl (Plates

21, 22) in which this same hieroglyph is many times repeated.

It is interesting to observe that the centre of the volutes of the smoking mirror is a dead man's bone. This suggests that, like the unfolding flower at the tip of Quetzalcoatl's shinbone emblem (Fig. 50), the starry volutes representing Venus symbolize the spiritual life engendered by the sacrifice of perishable matter. In an Aztec monument Tezcatlipoca's sign springs from the forehead of a skull which carries in its mouth the symbol of the "blossoming war" (Fig. 71). The scene in which Xolotl is being cooked in the kettle means just this. The symbol for detachment and of self-forgetfulness, nucleus of the Morning Star, is here represented as Xolotl's corpse. The "smoking mirror" seems thus to contain the whole doctrine of Quetzalcoatl, and the fact that this important hieroglyph symbolizes the message of the creator of man and all his universe points once

Fig. 71. Skull bearing the hieroglyphs *burning water* (issuing from the mouth) and *smoking mirror* (at the top of the skull). (Mexican National Museum.)

72

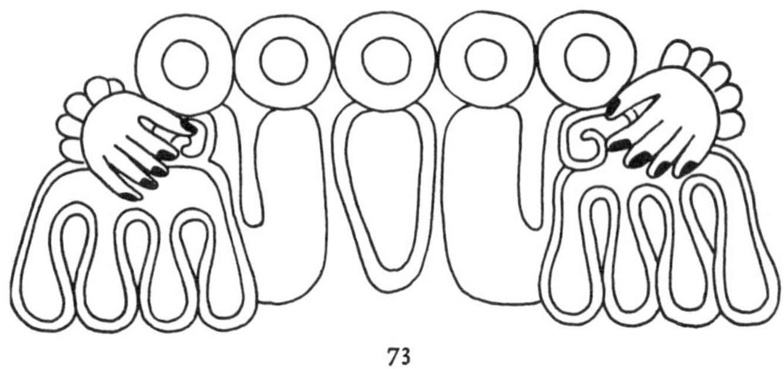

73

Fig. 72. Hand of God, from a Teotihuatecan fresco.

Fig. 73. Hands are the central motif in Teotihuacan. The drops falling from them always appear in respresentations of hearts. (Teotihuatecan fresco.)

again to Tezcatlipoca as being the representative of the human race.

This god carries the mirror in place of the foot that has been torn off by the Earth Monster. Since Tezcatlipoca personifies the nocturnal or terrestrial sun, we presume that this mutilation expresses the fact that every time it makes its journey across the

Fig. 74. Divine footprint on a Teotihuatecan vase. (Collection Kurt Stavenhagen.)

earth the sun abandons a small piece of itself: the missing foot is all the infinite number of divine particles sown in the bosom of mortal men, and the mirror with its clouded surface must be the symbol of the world of forms which, according to Nahuatl mysticism, is but a reflection of hidden reality. Could there be an image more perfectly suited to the humanity of the Centre than this mirror smoking like an evaporating lake, a lake whose substance, set in motion by heat, rises to heaven? And is it not precisely the image of the burning water which symbolizes the hard human task of transcending the earthly state?

Tezcatlipoca has not been found in Teotihuacan in the same form in which he appears in later iconography. He may of course be hidden somewhere in the ninety per cent so far unexplored; however, since the most salient characteristic of the Lord of the Smoking Mirror is that he is invisible, we think he may quite well have never been represented in the city which transmitted the tradition with such intense purity. The insistence of the texts upon Tezcatlipoca's invisibility shows how strongly this aspect of the god pervaded the whole myth. We know, for example, that the priest used to receive the penitent who came to confession with the following words:

Fig. 75. Footprint of the Invisible God on the face of a goddess. (Codex Borgia.)

Fig. 76. Hieroglyph *movement* with divine footprints. (Codex Borgia.)

Fig. 77. Divine footprints marking out the route the Aztec tribes must take. (Pilgrim frieze.)

> ". . . Lay thyself bare, cast out all thy shame in the presence of our lord who is called Tezcatlipoca. Thou art surely in his presence though thou art not worthy to behold him nor does he ever speak to thee because he is invisible and impalpable. . . ."[33]

The same kind of thing is said every time this god is invoked in his numerous aspects.

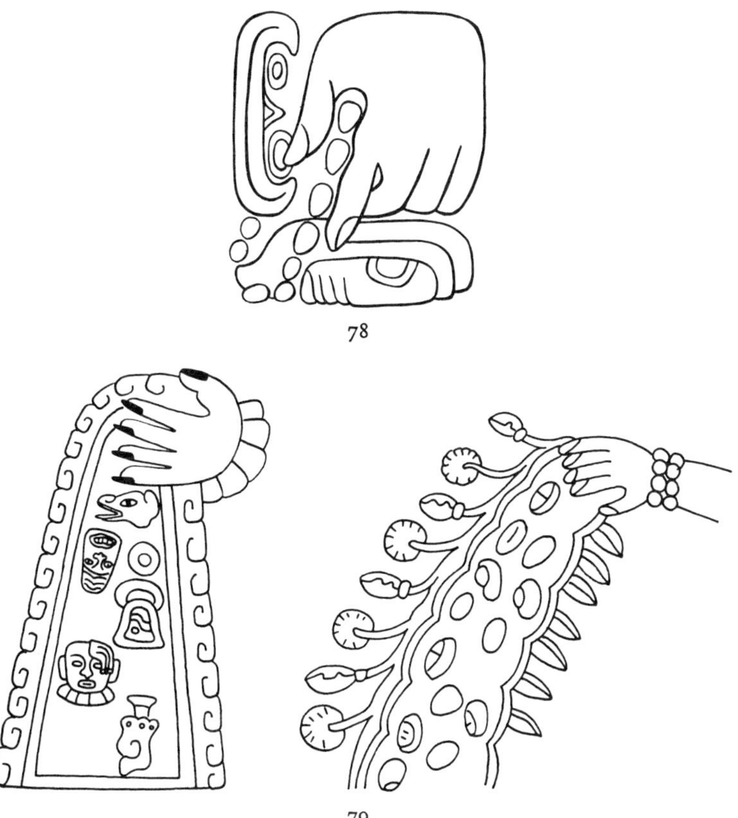

78

79

Fig. 78. The hand is an important Mayan hieroglyph. (Copán sculpture.)
Fig. 79. Objects flowing from miraculous hands. (Teotihuatecan fresco.)

There do exist in Teotihuacan hands (Figs. 72 and 73) and feet (Fig. 74), treated as central motifs. If we remember how exact a meaning there is in even the smallest of the symbols found there, we may conclude that these represent Tezcatlipoca in fragmentary form.

The iconography and the rituals leave no room for doubt that the invisible presence of the god is betrayed by the footprints. In the codices these footprints appear on the bodies of

Fig. 80. Deity creating the world of forms, which are seen pouring from his hands. (Teotihuatecan fresco.)

certain figures (Fig. 75) and in hieroglyphs (Fig. 76). They have clearly a much more important significance than the one usually attributed to them, according to which they refer to some purely physical act, such, for instance, as the march of the nomad tribes. The rites performed in the twelfth month to celebrate the arrival of the gods upon earth also throw light on this divine symbolism. Sahagún tells how:

> "... At midnight they ground a little maize flour and made a good thick mass of it; they made this mass of flour round like cheese, upon a rush mat. By this means they perceived when all the gods had arrived, because a small footprint appeared in the flour; then they understood that the gods had come. A priest ... remained waiting all night when this sign of the arrival of the gods was to appear, and he

Fig. 81. This Tiger-Bird-Serpent's breath (ear of tiger, bird feathers, and serpent-tongue) is covered with human hearts. (Teotihuatecan fresco.)

came and went many times an hour, to look at the mass, and when he saw the footprint in the flour, then that priest said: 'His majesty has come.' When the other priests and ministers of the idols heard the voice, they rose and played their conches and trumpets in every temple, in every district, and in every village. . . ."[34]

Obviously in such a serious art it would have been inconceivable to use one of those footprints—which had the power of so moving the multitude—for a profane end. The symbolism is in any case clear if we look at the graphic representations. It is easy enough to see, for example, that the Teotihuatecan figure (Fig. 42) cannot be analysed by the standards of positivism. His robes dotted with hieroglyphs, his sacrificial knife cutting out a heart, the temple atrium in which he is placed, show him to be an initiate, a priest in communion with the divine. How, before an expression of such concentrated holiness—an expression which implies an inner strength, a richness of invention, and a truly amazing artistic mastery—how, before such a refined mystical conception, can we possibly consider the footprints to be ingenuous representations of the dancer's steps during some ritual? Must they not rather represent the hidden divine presence?

It may be that the footprints in the later and inferior paintings depicting nomad marches really represent the same thing (Fig. 77). This is the more probable in view of the fact that all the chroniclers speak of Huitzilopochtli as being the Aztecs' guide during their long wanderings.

The sacred character of the hand is also clear. This hieroglyph appears frequently in Mayan sculptures and painted books (Fig. 78). It appears in Teotihuacan, not only as a separate entity, but also on certain figures full of a symbolism that shows a high creative power. Like the breath issuing from the mouth (Fig. 31), the streams of signs flowing miraculously from the hands (Fig. 79) must indicate the vital energy the gods impart to mortal men. In spite of the materialistic interpretations, these fountains of objects pouring from the hands of mythical beings (Fig. 80) irresistably invoke the idea of Creation: they must in fact represent the act of sowing, but a sowing in which the seeds are the whole universe of humanity. So in these scenes the gods are caught in the act of giving breath to the world of forms, of transforming their hidden reality into visible phenomena. Each object that flows from their hands is simply the outer covering for some celestial particle.

The symbolism of the fluid flowing from the hands seems to occur only in the City of the Gods. The symbol of breath, however, spread throughout Meso-america and persisted down to the time of the Spanish conquest. Although, following in Seler's footsteps, investigators would like to interpret these volutes as representing the physical word, they seem to have a spiritual significance. Possibly they represent something like the creative energy latent in the figures from which they issue. In this connexion it is significant that the sign on the volutes issuing from the mouth of the tiger-bird-serpent (which, it will be remembered, symbolizes the reuniting of the three cosmic spheres), represent the human heart (Fig. 81). We need not multiply examples, but will confine ourselves only to the images we have already seen: the eagles and tigers on the Aztec drum (Fig. 33) and the stone eagle commemorating the founding of Tenochtitlan (Fig. 20), both of which breathe out the sign of the burning water, which contains their message.

Whatever we may think of these interpretations, it is certain that the most superficial analysis reveals the sacred nature of every one of the signs that compose this symbolic language. For example, the linking of the hand and foot with the mystic number 5,[35] and with the precious stones (Fig. 82) is sufficient to convince us that these images cannot possibly belong to profane beings. They must, then, reveal the presence in Teotihuacan of the invisible god, the all-powerful Tezcatlipoca.

Fig. 82. Hand and foot in a composition whose divine nature is revealed by the cipher 5 and the precious stones. (Teotihuatecan fresco.)

NOTES

1. *Anales de Cuauhtitlan*, op. cit., p. 9.
2. Angel María Garibay, *Historia de la Literatura Nahuatl*, op. cit., Vol. I., p. 311.
3. Sahagún, op. cit., Vol. II, p. 278.
4. *Ibid.*, p. 164.
5. Laurette Sejourné, *Revista Mexicana de Estudios Antropológicos*, Mexico, 1956.
6. Alfonso Caso, *El Pueblo del Sol*, op. cit., p. 72.
7. Sahagún, op. cit., Vol. I, p. 23.
8. *Ibid.*, p. 385.
9. Confirmation of this hypothesis lies in the fact that these shells are all decorated with the symbol of the cycle of time (Fig. 51). To judge from their number and quantity, the rôle played by this instrument in the City of the Gods must have been of great importance. It is interesting to observe that even in our day the harsh sound of seashells holds sway over the ritual of some remote tribes. (Sejourné, *Supervivencias de un mundo mágico*, Fondo de Cultura Económica, Mexico, 1953.)
10. Because of his haste and his fear of death, this visit to the infernal regions reminds us of the dangers against which the dead soul guards himself, saying: ". . . Ye must pass between two mountains that meet . . ." Sahagún, op. cit., Vol. I, p. 315. In both cases the reference is undoubtedly to a rite symbolizing the passing into a new spiritual order.
11. Anales de Cuauhtitlan, op. cit., p. 11.
12. Sahagún, op. cit., Vol. I, p. 319.
13. *Ibid.*, Vol. II, p. 309.
14. *Ibid.*, Vol. I, p. 187.
15. *Ibid.*, p. 42.
16. *Ibid.*, p. 42.
17. *Ibid.*, p. 43.
18. *Ibid.*, p. 43.
19. *Ibid.*, p. 136.
20. *Ibid.*, p. 147.
21. Carl Lumholtz, *Unknown Mexico*, Charles Scribners Sons, New York, 1904, p. 301.

22. Sahagún, op. cit., Vol. I, pp. 138-40.
23. *Ibid.*, p. 140.
24. Sahagún, op. cit., Vol. I, p. 190.
25. It is doubtless the joyful character of this triumphal march that attaches to Xochipilli the attributes of the god of games and feasting.
26. We note that the attributes of Huitzilopochtli are the same as those of Xochipilli, Lord of Souls. In either case the symbolism—fire and the humming-bird—is that of resurrection.
27. Sahagún, quoted by Seler on p. 254.
28. Sahagún, op. cit., Vol. I, p. 287.
29. Eduard Seler, *The Tonalamatl of the Aubin Collection*, Berlin and London, 1900, p. 114.
30. Justino Fernández, *Coatlicue*, Centro de Estudios Filosoficos, Mexico, 1954.
31. Sahagún, op. cit., Vol. I, p. 102.
32. *Ibid.*, pp. 148-52.
33. Sahagún, op. cit., Vol. I, p. 33.
34. *Ibid.*, p. 204.
35. If 5 is the number of dynamic meeting, abolishing opposites, then seven, associated with scenes of plenty (Fig. 32), may represent the final reintegration into the *great whole*.

CONCLUSION

We need not continue our lists of gods, for though there are still others of importance, such for instance as the god of pulque—a sacred drink which played an essential rôle in Initiation—in analysing them we should merely have to apply the general principles so frequently found throughout this study, for the complex ideas of this religious system rest upon one central thought raised to the status of a law. This thought is perfectly defined by the very name of the Nahuatl Era (that of *Ollin Tonatiuh*, the Fifth Sun), because we know that the term *movement* (Ollin) describes that particular human activity whose object is to overcome inertia. Liberation from the weight which drags downward toward death is only possible if close watch is kept over the fiery particle each person carries within him; that is why man, whose conscious actions can transfigure matter, is transformed in this system into a demigod. Gravity and inertia are replaced by the spiritual law of ascent, of the creative impulse.

In the sensible universe represented by the symbols, the planets are the only bodies possessed in visible form of this prodigious energy which opens up a way of escape from destruction. Brilliant symbol of the great hidden truth, the Sun daily points out to man the way of salvation. Like all creation, the Sun is regulated by the law of gravity. Nevertheless at every dawn he leaves his nightly prison to rise resolute toward his luminous maturity. Thus in the drama revealed by Quetzalcoatl the different phases of the Sun's course represent the various spiritual categories which co-exist in human beings; and it is because of the transcendent symbolism of heavenly phenomena that astronomic cycles are so important. We have seen that Aztec society lived through its final years in the certainty that it had reached the end of a cycle. Moreover the discourse Moctezuma delivered to Cortés is proof that the deep-rooted belief in Quetzalcoatl's second coming actually signified the advent of a new age. Since Quetzalcoatl abandoned his country in order to save human kind from a contradiction, his return can only reasonably take place when synthesis has been achieved and the reign of peace replaces the "blossoming war". From this it follows that the change of cycle implied the advent of a new spiritual order.

There is nothing that would help us to penetrate deeper into Pre-columbian thought more than an exact knowledge of the astronomical basis of these temporal cycles within which the whole universe, having sounded a common note, advances a step further toward ultimate freedom. A study of this kind might help more than anything else to restore its lost brilliance to this ancient spirituality.

The planets symbolize the process of the transfiguration of matter: their revolutions are illustrated by the gods they are associated with, and whose distinguishing ornaments and rituals embody the doctrine which teaches mankind how to reach step by step to higher levels of freedom. Each of the Nahuatl gods is therefore an actor whose rôle is rigorously determined by the dramatic needs of the whole: leading characters together with those of lesser importance exist only for the sake of the complete plot. Therefore an analysis of all the gods becomes monotonous; they all belong to the same plot, and this plot soon becomes clear, especially since the subtleties of each character must be subordinated to the whole.

We are painfully aware of having described the symbolic language only sketchily; but it would have been impossible, without giving rise to unnecessary confusion, to study each separate image in this grandiose religious system. We confess to feeling incapable of describing the vision of the Nahuatl world which we have glimpsed in the course of our work. We sincerely hope that others, more competent or more inspired, will one day be able to do it greater justice. We have not lightly become convinced that it would be hard to find a poem more revealing of the inner life or purer in form than the one which inspired the message of Quetzalcoatl.

INDEX

References to line drawings are indicated by page numbers in italic type.

Acosta, Jorge, 127
Amantecas (*see* featherwork)
Amantla, 132
American historians, Congress of, 83
Annals of Cuauhtitlan, quotations from: 40, 56–8, 62, 98, 131, 142
Astronomy, Toltec knowledge of, 23; cycle of time, 89, *138*, 180, Plate 7
Atlatl, Nahuatl weapon, 106
Atl-tlachinolli, meaning of, 105
Azcapotzalco, 11
Aztec Empire, 1–46; fall of, 3, 43–6; nature of society, 6–11; totalitarian state, 14, 30; formation of culture, 18–21; boundaries of, 24; lack of religious belief in, 28; political motives in, 34; carvings and monuments in, *92, 107, 119,* Plate 9

Baptism, ceremony of, 9–11, 61, 136
Blossoming war, 72, 105, 108, *119,* 121, 150, 158, 183
Burning water, *108, 109,* 110, 160–161, *171*
Butterflies, symbolizing fire, 104; stylizations of, *106;* and soul, 142

Calmecac (*see* College of Princes)
Calpulco, place for disposing of bodies, 29
Capital punishment, in Aztec society, 15
Caso, Alfonso, 116; quotations from, 26, 90, 123, 135
Centre, law of (*see* Fifth Sun)
Ceramics, various types, 98, *99, 116, 147, 151, 155, 173*
Chalchiuhtlicue (*see* Waters, goddess of)
Chantico, earth goddess, 160, *161*
Chavero, Alfredo, 35
Chichimeca, nomad tribes, 18, 176; boundaries of, 24; speaking Nahuatl, 36; wars of, 37; established on plateau, 45
Chimalpaín, native chronicler, 17
Cholula, slaughter of, 2
Cinteotl, son of corn goddess, 152
Coatlicue, mother of Huitzilopochtli, 158–61, Plate 20
Codex Borbonicus, Venus and Soul in, 59; Cross of Quetzalcoatl in, *96;* hieroglyph *movement* in, *97;* Earth Sun and Quetzalcoatl in, *113,* Quetzalcoatl in *131;* Tezcatlipoca in, *162, 163*
Codex Borgia, hieroglyph *movement* in, *97, 145;* tree of, 117, *123,* 147; Quetzalcoatl as wind god

in, *135, 141;* Xolotl in, *149;* footprints in, *174*
Codex Dresden, 168
Codex Florentine, *95, 97, 111*
Codex Magliabeci, *137*
Codex Nuttal, *114, 121*
Codex Ramirez, quotation from, 19
Codex Vindobonensis, *123*
College, Aztec, 8; of Princes, 26–27; aim of, 72; and Temple of Quetzalcoatl, 87
Communion, sacrament of, 60–16
Confession, among Aztecs, 9–11, 61
Copán sculpture, 175
Corn god, feast to, 13; Cinteotl as, 152
Cortés, Hernán, conquers Mexico, 1; narrative of, 16; and Moctezuma, 38–43, 182; quotations from, 5–6, 42–3
Cosmology, Nahuatl, 86; cosmic levels, *121*
Coyolxauhqui, 160, Plate 19
Coyote, 111, *113*, 131
Creation, myths of, 55; human behaviour and, 118
Cremation, 127
Cross, symbol of, 73; as quincunx, 89–96, *91, 95, 96,* 102, 140, 153, *153*
Cuauhtemoc, surrender of, 3; heroism of, 45; meaning of, 47; sun called, 112
Cuicuilco, earliest Meso-american temple, 80–1
Cuitláhuac, massacre in, 40

Díaz del Castillo, Bernal, narrative of, 16; quotations from, 5, 12
Discourse, to adolescents entering College, 8
Dolls, children's, 23, 133, Plate 14
Dreamers, massacre of, 42

Eagle, sun as, *107,* 112, 121, 140; struggle with tiger, *114,* solar, *115;* representing blossoming war, *119;* descending, 161–2 (*see* also Cuauhtémoc)
Eyes, significance of diseases of, 150; rhomboid, *102*
Earthly Paradise (*see* Tlalocan)

Featherwork, Toltec, 22, 130–2
Female images, 50, 52, 133, Plate 13
Fernández, Justino, 161
Fire, union of water and, 99–110; rain of, 112
Fire god, named Xiuhtecutli, 30; first appearance of, 80; "earth's umbilicus", 91; quincunx on headdress of, *91;* picture of ceremony, *96;* characteristics of, *102;* statue of, *105;* sacrifice to, 156; symbol of resurrection, 181
Flaying, 148–56 (*see* also Xipe-Totec)

Flowers, in Nahuatl literature, 72; Lord of, 117–18; spiritual meaning of, 144–8
Foot, mirror replacing, 172–3; prints of, *173, 174,* 176–7, *179*
Forms, world of, *176*
Frazer, Sir James, 49
Frog, Lord of Earth, 135

Garibay, Angel María, quotations from, 3–4, 7–8, 61–4, 69–70, 72, 132
Gods, Nahuatl, 130–83

Hacienda, Mexican Department of, 98
Hands, in Teotihuacan, *172,* 175, *175, 176,* 178, *179*
Heart, and prickly pear, 105; representations of, *124, 125, 127, 172;* and penitence, 119–27; uplifting of, 131; from skeleton, 137; blossoming, 147; in mouth of Tiger-Bird-Serpent, 178 (*see also* Human Sacrifice)
Heaven and Hell, union of, 111–119
Heavenly heart (*see* Fifth Sun)
Huastecan statue, 170
Huehueteotl (*see* Fire, god of)
Huemac (*see* Lord of the Land of the Dead)
Huicholes, 152
Huitzilopochtli, Aztec hero, 19, 178; only Aztec deity, 29; and sacrifice, 31; house of, 40; symbology in life of, 56; ceremony of receiving his body, 60; and flower offerings, 144–6; Fifth Sun and, 156–61; sister of, 160; and Tezcatlipoca, 166; and resurrection, 181
Human sacrifices, 11–16, 29–34, 37; knives for, *125, 126, 127, 128;* none to Huitzilopochtli, 145–6; south sacrificed to Tezcatlipoca, 163–6
Humming bird, symbol of resurrection, 157, 181; and migrating Aztecs, 158

Ihuimécatl, a demon, 56–7, 62
Ixtlilxochitl, native chronicler, 17, 36; quotations from, 24, 31–3, 36–8
Ioallaoa, 154

Jiménez Moreno, Wigberto, quotation from, 17–18

King of Tollan, 27, 64, 71, 73, 75, 83, 111, 136, 142
Knights Eagle and Tiger, order of, 68, 115, *116, 117, 118,* 153, Plate 8

Land of Birth, 71
Land of the Dead, Quetzalcoatl's descent into, 54, 69, *143*
Lord of Dawn, 124, 139, Quetzalcoatl transformed into, 142
Lord of Earth, *134,* 134–5

Lord of the Land of the Dead, 41, 137

Lord of Liberation (*see* Xipe-Totec)

Lord of the Year, 91

Lumholtz, 152

Magic, 48–53; representations of humans and animals, 80

Maize, discovery of, 26; importance of, 52

Malinalxochitl, sister to Huitzilopochtli, 19

Malinalco, Plates 10, 11

Marquina, Ignacio, 86, 127

Masks, importance of, 130, from Teotihuacan, 134; wind-god and, 141, Plate 15

Maya, cities of, 81, 88; Cross of Kan and, *95;* Venus and, *96, 167, 168,* 170; tree, 116, Plate 12; hands in symbology of, *175,* 178; sculptured stone, Plate 12

Mazapan (*see* Ceramics)

Mexican National Museum, no Toltec room in, 127; head of Huitzilopochtli's sister in, 159–160; illustrations of works from, *93, 95, 105, 107, 116, 129, 134, 138, 151, 171;* quotation from Annals of, 82

Mexico, conquest of, 1–6

Michoacan, kingdom of, 24

Mictlantecuhtli (*see* Lord of the Land of the Dead)

Mixtecas, 36, 118

Moctezuma, rebellion against, 2; palace of, 6; adept at betrayal, 33; and Tlahuicole, 34; and disintegration of Aztec Society, 38–45; discourse to Cortés, 182

Monte Alban, Oaxaca, *170*

Moon, in legend of suns, 76–7

Morning Star, 141–2, *141, 165,* 166, *167, 168, 169*

Movement, sign of, 93, *97, 106,* 114, 118; sun of, 124, 157–8; hieroglyph, *128, 145, 174*

Muñoz Camargo, Diego, 34, quotations from, 68, 126

Mysteries, of initiation, 66–8, 76, 146, 154, 177, 182; and Mayan tree, 116; of Cosmic Passion, 166

Nahuas, language of, 3, 17, 36; founders of Pre-Columbian Mexican religious system, 21; influence of, 24; knew of god creator, 35; symbolic language of, 80–129; antiquity of, 82–3; cosmology of, 86; hieroglyphs of, *95;* gods of, 130–83

Nanautzin, god who sacrificed himself, 75

Netzahualcoyotl (Netzahualcoyotzin), and taking life, 32–3, 35; adept of Quetzalcoatl's religion, 36–7

Newborn, words recited to, 55–6

Numerology, of number five, 89, *179,* 191; of nine and twelve, *138*

Ollin, meaning of, 158, 182

Palenque, sculpture from, Plate 12
Parsons, Clew, 50; quotation from, 51
Penitence, confessor's discourse for, 9, 173–4; and Quetzalcoatl's teaching, 27–8, 64, 67; heart and, 119–27; symbol of, *129*, 139, 169; chrysalis born of, 142, Xolotl and, *145;* Xipe Totel and, 148–56 (*see also* Xolotl)
Pilgrim's freize, 174
Plumed Serpent, image of Quetzalcoatl, 25; not earlier than Teotihuacan, 83; sign of revelation, 84; on fresco, 102; image of consciousness, 114; metamorphosis of, 131
Prayer, in Quetzalcoatl's teaching, 27; Quetzalcoatl Lord of, 64; for spirituality, 151–2
Pregnancy, announcement of, 55
Prickly pear, and human heart, 105
Priesthood, institution of, 25; election to, 27; high priest as Quetzalcoatl, 30; foundations of a, 64
Pueblo Indians, 50
Pulque, god of, 182
Pyramid of Sun, 86, and Plate 1

Quaquauhtzin, killed by Netzahualcoyotl, 33
Quaxolotl, of divided head, 160
Quetzalcoatl, 24–46; god of life, 26; doctrine of, 35; maker of all creatures, 40; rebirth of his tradition, 43; religion and myth of, 53–77; "given his body", 56, 131; pilgrimage of, 60, *112;* builds a bridge, 66; as redeemer, 69; unchallenged position of, 85; temple of, 86–7, Plates 2, 3, 4, 5; and Era of Centre, 90–4; cross of, *95, 96, 101;* Annals of Cuauhtitlan, 98; message of, 108, 119, 157; Aztec monument of, 109; as Lord of Dawn, *110, 126;* in animal form, *113;* on Codex Borgia, 117, *122;* saved man from death, 118; and Earth Sun, 120; symbols on, 124; cremation and, 128; as penitent, *131;* breathing life into skeleton, *135;* as god, 136–43; as wind god, *137;* in Teotihuacan, *139, 140, 141;* as larva, *143;* movement from incarnation to spirit, 144; passion of, 150, 166; Tezcatlipoca and, 169; his double, 170; Huastecan statue of, 170, Plates 21, 22; shinbone of, 171; drama of, 182–3
Quetzalpetatl, Quetzalcoatl sleeps with, 57
Quinatzin, first king of Tezcoco, 36
Quincunx (*see* Cross)

Rain god (*see* Tlaloc)

Resurrection, symbol of, 157; feast of, 162; Huitzilopochtli and, 181
Rituals to the gods, 12–13
Rivera, Diego, 146

Sacrifice, creation and, 59; of gods, 76–7; composition expressing, 169
Sahagun, Fray Bernardino de, documentary work of, 17–18; prayers collected by, 36; description of maize ceremonies, 52; on transformation of princes, 67; and terrestrial paradise, 101–2; and Xipe, 150; and victim of sacrifice, 155–6; narrative of Sun's journey, 166; quotations from, 2–3, 8–13, 15, 22–3, 25, 27, 29–30, 55–6, 59–61, 64, 66–7, 73–7, 82–3, 85, 99–101, 104, 129, 136, 144–6, 148–52, 153–4, 156, 158–9, 162–5, 174, 176–7
Salt, feast to goddess of, 13
Seler, Eduard, and Teotihuacan, 83; and number five, 89; and "blossoming war", 105; and Xolotl, 170; interpretation of volutes, 178; quotations from, 65, 78, 118, 160
Sexual abstinence, 146
Shells, emblem of Quetzalcoatl, *138,* 138–9, 180
Shinbone, symbol of, *137,* 169, 171
Skeleton, breathing life into, 137
Skull, 171, *171*
Slaves, purchase of, 11–12
Smoking Mirror, *171;* Lord of (*see* Tezcatlipoca)
Souls, beginnings of, 55; symbolized, 56; journeying of, 58–9; and "blossoming war", 108; to sun, 110; patron of; 117; Xochipilli, Lord of, 144–8; escort sun, 144, 156
Spinden, H. J., quotation from, 25
Stavenhagen, Kurt, *153, 173*
Sun, fed by man's blood, 14, 29, 156; transmission of human energy to, 28; sacrifice of, 59; Venus and, 60, 74; bonds between individual and, 61; House of, 61–2; legend of the, 69–70, 72, 74–7, 170; as tiger, 71, *112;* gives life to universe, 76; orientation of temples to, 86–8; Fifth, 86–92, *90, 93,* 117, 136, 149, 156–9, 182; Flower of, *101;* eagle as, 107, *115, 124;* souls to, 110; incarnation of, 111–12; Earth Sun, *113,* 120; journey of, 144, 156–7, 161; created by sacrifice of Corn Goddess, 152; god of, 161; sacrificed youth as, 165; Tezcatlipoca as, 166; points to man's salvation, 182

Tamoanchan, 118, *123*
Techotlalatzin, King of Tezcoco, 36
Tecuzistecatl, and myth of Fifth Sun, 74, 76

Tenochtitlan, Cortés arrives at, 1, 42; Great Temple of, 2–3, 68, 109, *111*, 147; descriptions of, 4–6, 16; discipline in, 14; foundation of, 19–20; same gods as earliest Nahuatl capital, 21; plumed serpent in, 25; ethical ideal of, 27; degeneration of, 28; tributes, 30; and Tlaxcala, 31–4; Moctezuma received Cortés in, 42; as spiritual power, 44; resistance of, 45; priests in, 64; moral law in, 67; emblem of, 116; Huitzilopochtli and, 157

Teotihuacan, origins of, 81–9; meaning of name, 85; and Fifth Sun, 86, 159, geometry and astronomy of, 89–93; paintings of, 94–9, 101–2, 111, 115, 121, 142, 177; hearts in, 119, orientation of, 127; symbols of images in, 132; masks from, 134; vases from, 147; Tezcatlipoca in, 173, 179; hands in, 175, 178. Illustrations from, Plates 1, 2, 3, 6, 13, 14, 15; Figs. on pp. 90, 91, 93, 96, 97, 99, 100, 101, 103, 106, 110, 112, 115, 117, 118, 120, 125, 127, 128, 133, 134, 138, 139, 140, 143, 146, 147, 153, 155, 172, 173, 175, 176, 177, 179

Teotl, meaning of, 85

Terrestrial paradise, *100*, 101

Tezcatlipoca, feast to, 13; giving Quetzalcoatl his body, 156–7; flayed, 152; Lord of Smoking Mirror, 161–79, *162*, *163*, *165*; as sun, 166

Tezcoco, war between Tlaxcala and, 32; settlement of, 36–7

Tezozmoc, native chronicler, 15, 17; quotations from, 19, 20

Tiger, sun as, 111, *112*, 161; struggle with eagle, *114*; representing blossoming war, *119*; Venus emerging from jaws of, *170*

Tiger-bird-serpent, *120*, *176*, 178

Tlacapillachiualoya, meaning of, 78

Tlachitonatuih, Earth Sun, 71

Tlahuizcalpentecuhtli (*see* Lord of Dawn)

Tlalhuicole, hero of Tlaxcala, 34

Tlaloc, sacrifices to, 13, 15; at Teotihuacan, 87, Plate 5, and Fire, 99, 104; bearing cross of Quetzalcoatl, *101*; presiding over terrestrial paradise, *101*, painted in fresco, *106*, and Chalchiuhtlicue, 135

Tlalocan, the earthly paradise, 66–67

Tlazolteotl, goddess, 152

Tlatecuhtli (*see* Lord of Earth)

Tlatilco, archaic centre of, 51

Tlaxcala, blood tribute imposed on, 31–4

Tlillan Tlapallan, the burner, 58

Tollan, the legendary, 23; city of Quetzalcoatl, 25, 27, 45, 80–4;

degeneration of, 28; meaning of, 82 (*see also* Teotihuacan)

Toltécatl, gives Quetzalcoatl his body, 56–7

Toltecs, 21–4; Aztec religion derived from, 29; and Tezcoco, 36–7; Great Artificers, 74; Toltec Elegy, 97

Tonalamatl of Aubin, Aztec codex, 160

Totec, feast to, 13

Tree of life, 115, 117, *122,* 147; descendants of, 118

Tula-Hidalgo, 47, 83, 98, *99, 124,* 127

Turkey (*see* Xolotl)

Tzicquaquatzin, Mexican noble, 33

Tzompantecuctli, assassination of, 40, 43

Unity and duality, 63–4, 104, 138

Unplumed serpents, 134

Venus, transformation of Quetzalcoatl into planet, 54, 65, 71, 73, 124; represents soul, 58; and sun, 60, 74; and calendar, 89–90; sign of, *90, 96, 167;* goes underground, 111; Xolotl and, 170; emerging from tiger's jaws, *170;* and spiritual life, 171

Water, union with fire, 99–110; signs of, *103*

Water, goddess of, newborn offered to, 9; Aztec monument of, *107;* kin to Tlaloc, 135, Plate 16

Winds, god of, *135,* 136, *137, 141*

Witch, chief of Aztecs, 19

Xicotencatl, noble of Tlaxcala, 32

Xipe-totec, feast to, 29; Lord of Liberation, 148–56, *151, 153, 155;* and Huitzilopochtli, 158; sword of, 169; Plate 18

Xiuhtecutli (*see* God of Fire)

Xochimilco, accused of espionage, 44

Xochipilli, Lord of Flowers and Souls, *111,* 117–18, 144–8, *146, 147,* Plate 17; in Codex Borgia, *122;* painted red, 148; and Cinteotl, 152; and Huitzilopochtli, 181

Xolotl, the dog, 71; refused death, 77; Quetzalcoatl's double, 79, 170; Codex of, 82; as chrysalis, 142; *143;* as penitent, *145, 149* burst eye of, 150; and Fifth Sun, 158–9; turkey, 162; or Great Xolotl, 166; cooked in kettle, 170–1

Zapotec Indians, 50; rituals dramatizing Quetzalcoatl's life, 65; cities of, 81; ceramics, *151;* hieroglyph of Morning Star in art of, *169*